Tips for the Mathematics Teacher

**CORWIN
PRESS**

The Corwin Press logo—a raven striding across an open book—represents the happy union of courage and learning. We are a professional-level publisher of books and journals for K–12 educators, and we are committed to creating and providing resources that embody these qualities. Corwin's motto is "Success for All Learners."

Tips for the Mathematics Teacher

Research-Based Strategies to Help Students Learn

Alfred S. Posamentier
Hope J. Hartman
Constanze Kaiser

CORWIN PRESS, INC.
A Sage Publications Company
Thousand Oaks, California

For information:

Corwin Press, Inc.
A Sage Publications Company
2455 Teller Road
Thousand Oaks, California 91320
E-mail: order@corwinpress.com

CORWIN
PRESS

SAGE Publications Ltd.
6 Bonhill Street
London EC2A 4PU
United Kingdom

SAGE Publications India Pvt. Ltd.
M-32 Market
Greater Kailash I
New Delhi 110 048 India

Printed in the United States of America

Library of Congress Cataloging-in-Publication Data

Posamentier, Alfred S.
    Tips for the mathematics teacher: Research-based strategies to help students learn /
 Alfred S. Posamentier, Hope J. Hartman, Constanze Kaiser.
        p. cm.
    Includes bibliographical references and index.
    ISBN 0-8039-6589-3 (cloth: acid-free paper).—ISBN   0-8039-6590-7 (pbk. : acid-free paper)
    1. Mathematics—Study and teaching. I. Hartman, Hope J. II. Kaiser, Constanze. III. Title.

    QA11.P61764 1998
    510'.71—dc21   97-45401

This book is printed on acid-free paper.

03 10 9 8 7 6 5 4 3

Production Editor: Sherrise M. Purdum
Production Assistant: Denise Santoyo
Editorial Assistant: Kristen L. Gibson
Typesetter/Designer: Marion Warren
Indexer: Pilar Wyman
Cover Designer: Marcia M. Rosenburg

Contents

Contents

Introduction

Educational research, often conducted at universities or on educational sites by university researchers, is reported in educational journals, and is most often read by other researchers. The community of classroom teachers, which could benefit enormously from the findings of much of these educational initiatives, rarely learns about these endeavors. It is the objective of this book to bring some of the more useful research findings to the classroom teacher. Rather than to merely present the research findings, we have attempted to translate them into useful classroom tips.

This book should serve as a resource for mathematics teachers. It should provide these teachers with a way to access the many worthwhile findings resulting from educational, psychological, and sociological research studies done in Europe and in the United States. Heretofore, teachers have had no proper vehicle for getting this information—short of combing through the tomes of research reports in the various disciplines. This book is designed to provide an easy way for the classroom teacher to benefit from the many ideas embedded in these otherwise academic exercises.

The format of the book makes it an easy and ready reference for the mathematics teacher. The book consists of four chapters, each with a theme representing one aspect of the typical instructional program.

Each chapter presents a collection of teaching tips, concisely presented in a "friendly" format:

- **THE TIP:** A simple or crisp statement of the teaching tip.

- **What the Research Says:** A discussion of the research that led to the tip. This section should simply give the teacher some confidence in, and a deeper understanding of, the principle being discussed here as a "teaching tip."

- **Classroom Applications:** This describes to the teacher how this teaching tip can be used in the mathematics instructional program. Where appropriate, some illustrative examples of the teaching tip in the mathematics classroom are provided.

- **Precautions and Possible Pitfalls:** These are offered to make possible a reasonably flawless implementation of the teaching tip; that is, ways are presented to avoid common difficulties before they occur.

- **The Sources:** These are provided so that the reader may refer to the research to discover in more detail the process and findings.

We see this book as a first step in bringing educational research findings to practitioners—the classroom teachers. Perhaps teachers will see that there is much to be gained from reviewing educational research with an eye toward implementing the findings in their instructional program. Furthermore, it would be desirable for researchers to make more of an effort to extend their publications/findings to the classroom teacher. To do otherwise would make the entire activity of educational research irrelevant!

About the Authors

 **Alfred S. Posamentier** is Professor of Mathematics Education and Deputy Dean of the School of Education of the City College of the City University of New York. He is the author and coauthor of numerous mathematics books for teachers and secondary school students. As a sought-after guest lecturer, he favors topics regarding the teaching of mathematics in the best way possible, as well as aspects of mathematics problem solving and enrichment. He believes that teachers should use methods and materials that build on their individual strengths, rather than on a prescribed "best way to teach" in general. His popular book, *Teaching Secondary School Mathematics: Techniques and Enrichment Units* (1998), is built on this philosophy, as is this book on *Tips for the Mathematics Teacher*, which complements his earlier publication in that it is based on research, whereas the other book is not. After completing his A.B. degree in mathematics at Hunter College of the City University of New York, he took a position as a teacher of mathematics at Theodore Roosevelt High School in the Bronx (New York). During his 6 years in that position, he focused his attention on the teaching process in general and the improvement of students' problem-solving skills in particular. During this time he earned an M.A. degree from City College. Immediately on joining the faculty of the City College in 1970, he began to develop inservice

courses for secondary school mathematics that were practical in nature, and in which educational research could find its real value—when it was brought to the classroom teacher in the form of useful teaching tips. These courses were quite popular, drawing teachers from outside the usual attendance area. He received his Ph.D. from Fordham University (New York) in mathematics education and since has extended his reputation to Europe. He is an Honorary Fellow at South Bank University (London, England). He has been a visiting professor at several European universities—the Technical University of Vienna, Humboldt University at Berlin, and has been a Fulbright professor at the University of Vienna. He is often cited for his outstanding teaching. He was recently named Educator of the Year by the City College Alumni Association and on May 1, 1993, had a "day" named in his honor by the City Council President of New York City. More recently, he was awarded the Grand Medal of Honor from the Federal Republic of Austria and the Medal of Distinction from the City of Vienna (Austria). Now, after more than 28 years on the faculty of CCNY, he still exudes ever-increasing energy and enthusiasm for mathematics and mathematics education, making ever more contributions to the field in person and in print.

Hope J. Hartman is Professor of Education and Coordinator of Social and Psychological Foundations at the City College of the City University of New York. Her areas of specialization are improving thinking skills, improving attitudes that foster thinking, and using instructional methods that promote active learning. She earned her Ph.D. in cognitive psychology at Rutgers University. She received the Distinguished Paper Award from the Northeastern Educational Research Association. In the late 1970s, she served as Research Coordinator of a project of Special Services for Disadvantaged Students at Rockland Community College and instituted courses on logic and reasoning and effective listening. She worked as a research specialist for Newark, N.J., Public Schools in the early 1980s. In 1984, she became Assistant Director of a thinking skills program and Assistant Professor in the School of Education at Montclair State College. She has done extensive consulting for schools and districts in the northeastern United States. In 1986, she came to City College where she became Director of the former City College Tutoring and Cooperative Learning Program. She also served as Chair of the former Department of Secondary Education. She has done extensive faculty development with both public school teachers and college professors across the curriculum. She is the author of the book, *Intelligent Tutoring*, and several other works including journal articles, chapters, test reviews, and handbooks.

Constanze Kaiser, born in 1958 in what was then East Berlin, began her career as a teacher of mathematics and physics in 1982. She taught both subjects in high school for several years while also actively pursuing educational research. Both in her teaching and her research, her interest focused on the social interactions in the classroom between teacher and student. The subject of her first thesis was the analysis of students' internal representation of moral concepts in correlation with various situations. Her interest was focused on the individual student's role in the conventional school setting. In 1988, she completed her doctoral studies at Humboldt University, with a dissertation on investigations into the relationship between older students and teachers, wherein she performed quantitative and qualitative analyses of this relationship seen from the vantage point of common interests. While teaching in the 1980s, she investigated the literature and educational journals for helpful teaching tips to improve her work. Once at the university, she was constantly asked by students for practical tips that they could use in the classroom. Since 1993, she has concentrated her research on how male and female teachers read the body language of their students, and designs training programs for teachers on how to successfully read the body language of their students. On this topic, she has published several articles as well as a full-length book.

CHAPTER ONE

Instructional Techniques

THE TIP (1.1)

 Students need time to practice planning their solutions to problems.

What the Research Says

Students often have difficulty solving problems because they start working on a solution as soon as they finish reading a problem. Instead, they should try to understand the problem and then develop a problem-solving plan, like experts do. Students need to be taught the importance of planning the solving of problems and provided with time to practice planning their solution attempts. One study involved teaching a group of students to plan their problem solving in preparation for an exam they were going to take. Another group of students studied as they normally did for the exam. Students who were in the planning group performed better than those who used their traditional study methods, even though this group of students reported spending more time studying than did the students in the planning group.

Classroom Applications

The solution of a mathematics problem requires forethought, as indicated previously. One of the best ways to instill this trait in students is to model it in classroom activities. When tackling a problem with the class, rather than jumping right into solving it, the teacher should think out loud, allowing the students to follow the teacher's thought process on how he or she will solve the problem. Or, the teacher can conduct a discussion about how to go about finding a path to the solution. Students should see that planning must precede problem solving. Students also need a repertoire or "tool chest of problem-solving strategies" to apply to problems they are going to solve. Such strategies might include working backwards; finding a pattern; adopting a different point of view; solving a simple, analogous problem; using extreme cases; visually representing a problem; intelligent guessing; estimating and testing; accounting for all possibilities; organizing data; and logical reasoning. (For a detailed discussion of these problem-solving strategies, we recommend *Teacher! Prepare Your Students for the Mathematics for the SAT I: Methods and Problem-Solving Strategies* by A. S.

Posamentier and S. Krulik (Corwin, 1996) and *Problem-Solving Strategies for Efficient and Elegant Solutions: A Resource for the Mathematics Teacher* (Corwin, 1998).

In addition to planning to use such problem-solving strategies, other good planning techniques for students to use when solving mathematics problems include the following:

1. Ask students to represent (in pictures or symbols) and describe the problems they are solving (including what the relevant information is, what is irrelevant, what type of problem it is) and how they solve problems.

2. Have students compare their solution methods to those of an expert.

3. Have students compare how they solve one problem with how they solve other problems—some of which are similar and some of which are different.

4. Instead of having students carry out a solution, have them select a sequence of the operations needed to solve a problem. Have them refer back to the problem statement to make sure that the plan fits the problem.

Make sure students understand when, why, and where to apply mathematical procedures, concepts, algorithms, and strategies. Have students keep a journal in which they describe and evaluate their understanding of concepts and how they plan, monitor, and evaluate their problem solving. Journals should include descriptive and evaluative information. Descriptive information includes students' explanations of what their approach is: when, where, and why they used it for the particular problem, and how they used it. Evaluative information includes whether the approach was effective, if there is anything they would do differently next time, and if there are any other ways they could have solved the problem. Periodically collect the journals and give students feedback.

Precautions and Possible Pitfalls

 When demonstrating how to plan problem-solving approaches, be sensitive to students' different learning rates. Avoid rushing! Do not let the pace of the faster students push you to a speed that would be detrimental to slower students. If time is taken for proper modeling, the slower students can learn to master what you are teaching them about how to plan problem solving, and they might even learn this with a clearer understanding than the faster students. A rushed time factor could be quite harmful to all the students' learning patterns. Do not group problems into sets in which all the problems are solved the same way. This can create a problem-solving set, promote planning solutions by rote, and discourage thinking.

SOURCE

Nickerson, R. S., Perkins, D. N., & Smith, E. E. (1985). *The teaching of thinking.* Hillsdale, NJ: Lawrence Erlbaum.

THE TIP (1.2)

Emphasize the general principles that underlie solving specific types of problems.

What the Research Says

Many studies have shown that there are important differences between
experts and novices in how they solve problems. One important difference is that experts think about what principle could be applied to solve
a problem, whereas novices think about the superficial aspects of a problem.

In one study, 45 undergraduate physics students were classified into three
groups according to the reasons they gave when asked to compare 32 sets of 2
problems. For each set of problems they had to decide whether they would be
solved similarly. The "surface-feature" group consisted of students who used superficial aspects of the problems as the basis of their reasoning for at least 17 of the
32 sets of problems. The "principle" group consisted of students who used general
principles as the basis of their reasoning for at least 17 of the 32 sets of problems.
The "mixture" group consisted of students who used a wide range of reasoning
strategies, but none were used a majority of the time.

Next, students were given a problem-solving task consisting of four problems. This task also involved a mathematical proficiency task. The results showed
that the "surface-feature" group had the lowest level of performance, with a mean
of 14% correct. The "mixture" group's mean was 32% correct, and the "principle"
group had the highest level of performance, with a mean of 57% correct. These
findings suggest that principle use is related to success in problem solving. Other
studies have demonstrated that novices can be taught to think and solve problems
like experts.

Classroom Applications

Making students aware of strategies, or principles, relevant to problem
solving is one of the goals of the *Standards* of the National Council of
Teachers of Mathematics (NCTM). This can best be seen when observing students doing proofs in geometry. Typically, students observe the model
proofs presented by the teacher and then try to copy their example. Often this is
done with little or no thinking on the part of the student. Students know that prov-

ing triangles congruent, or similar, tends to lead to the desired result and, therefore, they simply do that with the hope that the next step will be the desired conclusion. Often, this proof is submitted as something that appears senseless. This
situation is an excellent opportunity to reinforce the strategy of "working backwards." Have the student go to the desired result (that which is to be proved) and
then ask how it can be proved. That is, if one supposes that the desired result was
to prove a pair of lines parallel, then one would seek to prove a pair of corresponding angles congruent or a pair of alternate-interior angles congruent, or some other
such relationship that can establish parallelism. Then, taking another step backwards, one asks how to get this pair of angles congruent—perhaps proving a pair
of triangles congruent. One then seeks to prove the triangles congruent and has to
select the proper method. And so it continues in a backwards-reasoning way. Once
the reverse path has been established, the proof is written in the forward order and
the proof is complete. This strategy, and especially an awareness of its existence,
will also go a long way to improving students' understanding of proofs and their
proof-writing ability.

Precautions and Possible Pitfalls

One must be aware that not all strategies can be successfully applied to
all problem situations. Sometimes, more than one strategy can be used
with equal facility. Other times, only one may be usable. The more
strategies that students are exposed to, the more powerful their problem-solving
skills will become.

SOURCES

Eylon, B., & Reif, F. (1984). Effects of knowledge organization on task performance.
    Cognition and Instruction, 1(1), 5-44.
Heller, J., & Reif, F. (1984). Prescribing effective human problem solving processes:
    Problem description in physics. *Cognition and Instruction, 1*, 177-216.
Thibodeau Hardiman, P., Dufresne, R., & Mestre, J. (1989). The relation between
    problem categorization and problem solving among experts and novices.
    Memory and Cognition, 17(5), 627-638.

THE TIP (1.3)

 Provide hints, clues, or ask "leading" questions when students need help solving problems, instead of giving them the answers. Gradually phase out this support to foster independent problem solving.

What the Research Says

The instructional technique of scaffolding is based on a concept known as the "zone of proximal development." This zone is the distance between what students can do when solving problems independently and what they can do when solving problems with someone who is at a higher level. Studies have shown that students who cannot solve problems on their own can often solve them if they are given temporary supports or "scaffolds" from another person who is more competent in the particular area. This person can be a teacher, parent, or another student. There are many different types of scaffolds that can be used, including hints, question prompts, partial solutions, and model solutions or worked-out examples. Working in groups solving problems cooperatively also provides scaffolding opportunities. These forms of support act as bridges between what students can do on their own and what they can do with guidance. As students make progress, these forms of support are gradually withdrawn. The result is that, eventually, students can solve the problems on their own.

Classroom Applications

The problems that arise when doing proofs in geometry often stem from the fact that students are more concerned with mimicking the teacher's model solution than with real comprehension. Through regular questioning, the teacher can systematically guide students through the proper "backwards method" for approaching a proof. These frequent and simple questions will eventually become part of the students' thinking process when doing proofs. Some sample questions (naturally, each teacher must do this questioning in his or her own words) include the following: What are we trying to prove? What are some of the ways we can establish this idea? How can we reach this previous statement? What are we given? Have we ever done a proof similar to this? And so on. Teachers should gradually reduce (and ultimately phase out) their questions as students begin to ask themselves the same sort of questions. To make sure this happens, follow the following steps:

1. Model self-questioning when problem solving by thinking aloud for students as you solve different types of problems. Make sure they see how you tailor the questions to the specific problem.

2. Give students guided practice self-questioning while solving different types of problems and give them feedback on their question formulation and use. Make sure students generate their own questions instead of just copying yours.

3. Have students independently practice self-questioning while solving a variety of problems, but have them write down their questions at each stage of the problem-solving process so you can give them feedback.

4. Remind students to continue to ask themselves questions while problem solving on their own, even though they won't be turning in the questions for your feedback.

After these four stages, students will eventually ask themselves questions automatically while solving problems, without having to think about it! This step-by-step gradual process of fostering independence should also be applied to giving students hints, clues, examples, partial solutions, and other scaffolds.

Precautions and Possible Pitfalls

 The guiding questions must be in the teacher's own words and be a direct response to the students' reactions. Care must be taken not to use prefabricated questions, independent of what is going on in the classroom—this would only create more confusion for the students.

SOURCE

Vygotsky, L. (1978). *Mind in society*. Cambridge, MA: Harvard University Press.

THE TIP (1.4)

 Computer-aided geometry lessons improve students' spatial abilities, especially that of girls.

What the Research Says

 Girls and boys do not differ in their abilities to do geometry. Girls and boys, however, use different strategies when solving geometry problems. Research on girls working with computers has shown the following:

1. Girls are more application oriented in their relationship to the computer.
2. Girls tend to offer theoretical concepts of solutions when first doing a programming problem.
3. When solving mathematical problems, girls' thinking is strongly guided by structural principles. In contrast, boys' thinking focuses on sequential solutions.

Overall, girls' ways of thinking enable a better working style for programming than boys. In comparison to boys, however, girls tend to shy away from computer science.

This study was conducted with 25 girls and 21 boys in two parallel eighth-grade classes. Students completed 10 lessons on "Special points and lines at the triangle." Although most recent research shows less sex differences in cognitive aspects of mathematical competence than in past research, spatial ability is an exception. Comparable research in 20 countries has shown sex differences related to geometry and measuring. Although there is no empirical proof of a causal relationship between good spatial ability and good performance in mathematics, it is evident that spatial abilities are an important factor.

From this point of view, it is interesting whether spatial abilities can be trained. Researchers investigated the question of whether ordinary geometry instruction (with a ruler and divider), or computer-aided geometry lessons, promoted more visible progress in spatial abilities. One class was taught by the classical geometry method (with a ruler and divider); the other class was taught using a computer-aided instructional program named Cabri Geometri. Students in both classes took a paper-and-pencil pretest and a posttest, which consisted of three parts:

Part 1. Identify figures

Part 2. Combination of cuboids

Part 3. Image to mirror figures

All geometrical facts were illustrated in just two dimensions. Comparison of pre- and posttest results demonstrates the possibility of improving spatial ability by training. In general, there were highly significant differences between pre- and posttests. Improved performance at posttesting was especially significant for tasks in Parts 1 and 2 of the test. There were no significant differences between pre- and posttest results for Part 3 of the test. These findings are valid for both classes combined as well as for each class individually. For the entire group (both classes combined), girls and boys did not differ in their pre- or posttest scores. There were significant differences between girls and boys in the class that received the computer-aided lessons. The girls learned more than boys did.

Classroom Applications

 Arrange exercises that correspond to the test.

1. Identify figures: Students see five similar figures, which differ only in a few details. Afterwards, students get 25 of these shapes. Students have to determine which of the five figures the 25 correspond to.

2. Combination of cuboids: Several small cubes are combined into one big one. This is shown in a drawing. Students have to find out for some of the small cubes how many other cubes they touch.

3. Image to mirror figures: Students have to mentally rotate a plane figure around a given axis. Then students have to select from a choice of four possibilities the one that meets the thought reflection.

In Task 3, spatial orientation plays a subordinate role, while the student's ability to estimate distances has an overriding importance. Math teachers should take into consideration, however, the spin-off of the investigation—that students have difficulties in estimating distances.

Precautions and Possible Pitfalls

 Although the research showed clear support for the computer as an instructional tool in geometry, do not consider the computer as a cure-all. Traditional instruction was also successful.

SOURCE

Reiss, K., & Albrecht, A. (1994). Unterscheiden sich Mädchen und Jungen beim Geometrielernen mit und ohne Computer? [Is there a difference between girls and boys concerning learning of geometry with and without computer?]. *Mathematica Didactica, 17*(1) 90-105.

THE TIP (1.5)

 Encourage students to make mental pictures while applying rules to solve problems.

What the Research Says

Creating and using mental images about rules can help students solve problems. A study was conducted with 52 ninth-grade students, who were assigned to one of two groups. Both groups were given information on Boyle's Law, Charles's Law, and Gay-Lussacs's Law. One group of students was encouraged to create mental images of a typical gas as it responded to different amounts of pressure, temperature, or volume. This group was also instructed to draw an image of this in their notebooks. Students in the other group were not instructed to make mental pictures or draw images in their notebooks. These students were told to write the rule and repeat it out loud while learning. After three days of instruction on the gas laws, students were given an exam and completed a questionnaire designed to assess their use of imagery while they were taking the exam. The exam consisted of two parts. The first part was made up of six multiple-choice items designed to measure students' memory. The second part consisted of six essay questions in which students had to use the rules to solve problems. Students had to solve these problems correctly and give acceptable explanations of their answers.

The results showed that the imagery group did better than the nonimagery group in solving the problems, but the nonimagery group did better than the imagery group on the memory part of the exam. Many other studies, however, have demonstrated that mental imagery can have a very beneficial impact on memory.

Classroom Applications

This research has clear implications for mathematics instruction. For learning algorithms, it makes sense to have students remember the rule being used. Perhaps later, a more in-depth study of the algorithm can be helpful. For the solution of problems, which, by their very nature do not call for a diagram, it is sometimes quite helpful to visualize the situation being described. Visualization can be in the form of sketches, diagrams, or mental pictures. A *mental picture* is a thought diagram. Consider the following problem:

In a room of 45 children, 28 wear eyeglasses, 30 are wearing a white shirt, and 5 are not wearing a white shirt and do not wear eyeglasses. How many are wearing a white shirt and have eyeglasses on?

To do this problem most expeditiously, it would be wise to mentally picture the students and draw a Venn diagram of the situation.

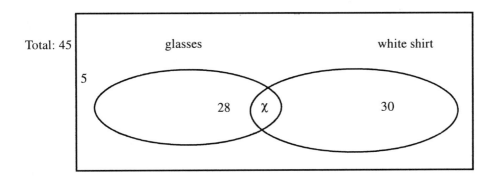

The intersection x can be found by the equation: $(28 - x) + (30 - x) + x + 5 = 45$, arrived at by adding the contents of each of the regions, which total 45. Therefore $x = 18$. Without drawing the diagram the problem would have been considerably more difficult. Nothing in the statement of the problem told the students to make the drawing. This is where the teacher's role is important. Teachers should directly instruct students in making drawings, mental pictures, or both of problems they are solving. Students need to be encouraged and reminded to make and use mental images and diagrams.

In addition to drawing, students can form mental pictures of problems just by using their visualization skills. For example, when reading a problem such as "Alicia is taller than Eama, and Michael is taller than Alicia. Who is the tallest?" a student can make mental pictures of Alicia, Eama, and Michael to compare their relative heights.

Precautions and Possible Pitfalls

Drawing pictures to represent abstract concepts or topics is useful but is by no means the solution to all problems. Teachers should be careful to make this point clear. Yet, they should always encourage students to try to represent the problem situation graphically so students might gain more insight. Many students view mental images as "crutches" or forms of cheating and feel guilty about using them. Let students know it's smart to use such strategies!

SOURCE

McIntosh, W. (1986). The effect of imagery generation on science rule learning. *Journal of Research in Science Teaching, 23*(1), 1-9.

THE TIP (1.6)

 Get students to "think out loud" when solving problems.

What the Research Says

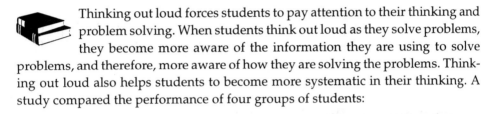 Thinking out loud forces students to pay attention to their thinking and problem solving. When students think out loud as they solve problems, they become more aware of the information they are using to solve problems, and therefore, more aware of how they are solving the problems. Thinking out loud also helps students to become more systematic in their thinking. A study compared the performance of four groups of students:

- Students who thought out loud with a specific mathematical problem-solving goal
- Students who thought out loud with a nonspecific mathematical problem-solving goal
- Students who thought silently with a specific goal
- Students who thought silently with a nonspecific goal

The "think out loud" groups were told, "Tell me, what equation are you going to look at or use? And why are you going to look at or use it?" The "think silently" groups were told, "Think about, what equation are you going to look at or use? And why are you going to look at or use it?" All groups were given a series of numeral conversion problems to solve with bases of 3, 4, 5, and 10, using four equations. Two days later they were given a written test designed to measure what they had learned during the problem-solving session. The results showed that students who thought out loud solved problems more efficiently with fewer unnecessary steps and with a more effective sequence of steps, but required more time to solve problems.

Classroom Applications

1. Have students work in pairs, with one thinking out loud while solving problems and the other listening analytically to how the problem is being solved. Rotate roles so all students serve as thinkers and listeners.

2. Think out loud for students as you solve problems to model for them how they should think about and solve problems. Purposely make mistakes so you can show students how to recover from errors.

Note: Let students know that smart people doing a mathematics problem—not only crazy people—talk out loud to themselves!

Precautions and Possible Pitfalls

1. People usually think faster than they speak, so sometimes thoughts trip over speech.

2. If students don't have adequate knowledge about the problem, they may not be able to think out loud about how they are solving it.

3. Students might be shy about thinking out loud because of cultural backgrounds, speech impediments, or simply peer pressure. Be aware of this issue.

SOURCES

Whimbey, A., & Lochhead, J. (1982). *Problem solving and comprehension*. Philadelphia, PA: Franklin Institute Press.

Zook, K. B., & DiVesta, F. J. (1989). Effects of overt, controlled verbalization and goal-specific search on acquisition of procedural knowledge in problem solving. *Journal of Educational Psychology, 81*(2), 220-225.

THE TIP (1.7)

 Before beginning a lesson, put an advance organizer outline of what you are going to cover on the blackboard.

What the Research Says

Learning is more meaningful when students know in advance what is going to be covered in a lesson and how the teacher organized the information to be learned. Seeing an outline on the board stimulates students' thinking about the various topics and helps them activate their prior knowledge about the topic. The connection between existing and new knowledge is an essential component of meaningful learning. The advance organizer also shows students how to organize information to be learned.

Classroom Applications

There is a very clever method of teaching the theorems in geometry that deal with the measurement of an angle related to a circle. As a first step, you might do a class on the various types of angles. Begin the lesson by putting an overview (advance organizer outline) of what you will be covering on the chalkboard. For example:

Theorems in geometry involving various types of angles related to a circle, beginning with the measurement of an inscribed angle:

A. An angle formed by two chords intersecting in the circle (not at the center)

B. An angle formed by two secants intersecting outside the circle

C. An angle formed by two tangent segments

D. An angle formed by a tangent and a secant

E. An angle formed by a chord and a tangent meeting at the point of tangency

Finding the relationship between the measure of an angle and the arcs it intercepts on a circle.

It is assumed that students have already learned that the measure of an inscribed angle of a circle is one-half the measure of its intercepted arc.

Begin by cutting out an appropriately large rectangular piece of cardboard and a cardboard circle. Staple two pieces of string to the rectangular cardboard, forming a convenient angle near the middle, and draw an angle of the same measure (as the angle formed by two pieces of string) as an *inscribed angle* of the circle.

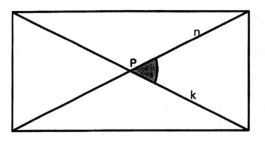

By moving the circle into various positions relative to the rectangle, all the theorems relating the circle to the different types of angles can be easily developed (and proved!).

1. An *angle formed by two chords intersecting inside the circle* has measure equal to one-half the sum of the intercepted arcs.

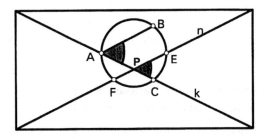

Place the circle so that $\overline{AB} \parallel n$ and $\overline{AC}$ is on k as in the figure above.

$$m \angle A = \tfrac{1}{2} m \ \overset{\frown}{BEC}$$
$$m \angle A = m \angle P$$

Therefore, $m \angle P = \tfrac{1}{2}m \ \overset{\frown}{BEC} = \tfrac{1}{2}(m\overset{\frown}{BE} + m\overset{\frown}{EC})$. But $m\overset{\frown}{BE} = m\overset{\frown}{AF}$, therefore,

$$m \angle P = \tfrac{1}{2}(m\overset{\frown}{AF} + m\overset{\frown}{EC}).$$

2. *An angle formed by two secants intersecting outside the circle* has measure equal to one-half the difference of the intercepted arcs.

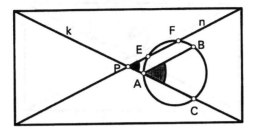

Place the circle so that $\overline{AB} \parallel n$ and $\overline{AC}$ is on k as in the above figure.

$$m \angle A = \tfrac{1}{2}\overset{\frown}{BC}$$
$$m \angle A = m \angle P$$

Therefore, $m \angle P = \tfrac{1}{2}m\overset{\frown}{BC} = \tfrac{1}{2}(m\overset{\frown}{FBC} - m\overset{\frown}{FB})$. But $m\overset{\frown}{FB} = m\overset{\frown}{AE}$; therefore,

$$m \angle P = \tfrac{1}{2}(m\overset{\frown}{FBC} - m\overset{\frown}{AE}).$$

A similar argument can be made for

3. An *angle formed by two tangents:*

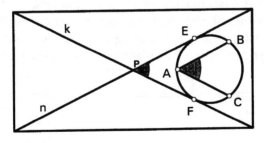

4. An *angle formed by a tangent and a secant:*

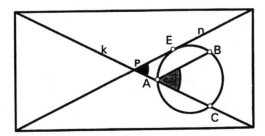

5. An *angle formed by a tangent and a chord:*

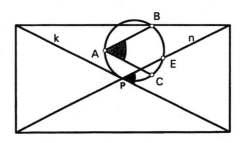

This advance organizer outline will stimulate students to think about what they already know about angles (e.g., what types of angles they know of—such as a triangle, have they ever heard of an inscribed angle, are they familiar with the concepts of tangents, secants, and so forth). It will also show students how you organize the ideas you are discussing—where one topic stops and another begins. You may want to include illustrations of each type of angle on the chalkboard so students can visualize the concepts and see whether or not they recognize them.

Precautions and Possible Pitfalls

As mentioned, this procedure for beginning a lesson has its advantages, but it also has the disadvantage of removing the "controlled surprise" factor from the lesson. It is important for the teacher to weigh this disadvantage against the gains when using this approach. Such professional judgments are always necessary when planning a lesson, but particularly in this case.

SOURCE

Ausubel, D. (1960). The use of advance organizers in the learning and retention of meaningful verbal learning. *Journal of Educational Psychology, 51,* 267-272.

THE TIP (1.8)

 Complex exercises, which give students freedom, tend to fit the way older students learn.

What the Research Says

 It is known that it can be difficult to keep older students motivated to learn. Some students plead for more challenging lessons, while others plead for more freedom. This study examined the conflict-loaded situation of older students.

The research investigated several ways to bridge the gap between students' urge for independence and the limitations of their abilities of self-control. One method of bridging this gap was investigated in this study. Students in the 10th grade were given a complex exercise. They were given the freedom and responsibility for using this exercise to prepare for a test. The results demonstrated higher motivation of students as well as higher achievement. The benefit was especially pronounced for students who were normally very quiet and reserved.

Classroom Applications

 This is one method of giving students freedom with exercises. Plan a period of complex exercises during which students have to apply varying knowledge as well as skills. Assignments in plane and solid geometry, or systems of equations are very suitable for such complex exercises because they present a variety of possible ways of solving a problem. In this complex exercise students have a variety of requirements, they receive instruction and get help from the teacher. The basic idea is to distribute lessons and priorities of the exercise.

The lessons (time line):

| | 1. | | 2. 3. 4. 5. | | 6. | | 7. 8. 9. | | 10. |

LP		Exercises	Interim Balance	Individual	Final Test
	ST	Basic Groups		ST Consolidation	

LP = Lesson for planning

ST = Short test

In the lesson for planning (LP), the goal of the exercise is explained and students are offered the chance to work according to their own standard. In Lesson 10, Final Test, every student selects 4 problems from a series of 10 problems of varying degrees of difficulty. In this way, each of the students demonstrates his or her willingness to make an effort and his or her learning progress. During the first exercise period (Lessons 2 to 5), most students are allowed to compose their own exercise program. At the end of a lesson, students have to make a note about the problems and experiences they had.

The basic group was made up of students with weak skills. They worked under direction of the teacher. In Lesson 6, the teacher and students strike an interim balance (an exchange of problems and experiences). According to the results of the short test, the teacher's observation, and student's self-assessment, the second exercise period is used

1. To strengthen basic mathematical knowledge for students with problems

2. For students to consolidate information by using a series of problems with increasing degrees of difficulty

3. For students who have already reached their goal and have the spare time to help other students

Lesson 10 becomes a sort of "moment of truth."

Precautions and Possible Pitfalls

If you plan such a unit, try to draw up a three-phase period as used in this example: exercise, balance, and consolidation. In the study cited, other numbers of phases did not provide the success that the three phases did and they were not as manageable.

SOURCE

Westphal, J. (1991). Unterricht mit Jugendlichen—Das Lernen älterer Schüler [Lessons with youth—The learning of older students]. *Pädagogik und Schulalltag, 46*(2), 224-230.

THE TIP (1.9)

 Use a Question-Asking Checklist and an Evaluation Notebook to help students become better learners.

What the Research Says

 Numerous studies have demonstrated that students often do not know what they don't know. Research has also shown that students can become aware of their strengths and weaknesses as learners, and can learn to take greater control over their own academic performance.

One such study was conducted with 64 students from two 9th-grade science classes and one 11th-grade biology class. There were four phases to this study:

Phase 1: Exploratory. This phase lasted 4 weeks and involved getting to know the students and seeking their consent for cooperation and participation in the rest of the study.

Phase 2: Awareness. This phase lasted 5 weeks for Grade 9 and 3 weeks for Grade 11. During this phase, students began thinking about themselves as learners. They reflected on their attitudes, learning difficulties, and strategies for overcoming these difficulties.

Phase 3: Participation. This phase lasted 7 weeks for Grade 9 and 6 weeks for Grade 11. Students began using the Question-Asking Checklist and the Evaluation Notebook. The teachers gave students a considerable amount of help using these materials during this phase.

Phase 4: Responsibility-control. This phase lasted 7 weeks for Grade 9 and 3 weeks for Grade 11. During this phase, the teachers' role virtually ceased and students used the materials on their own. Teachers monitored student behavior and attitudes and intervened only as needed.

Materials

Question-Asking Checklist: There were 10 different categories, each of which had its own icon and set of questions. The 10 categories included the following: topic, detail, task, approach, change in knowledge, increase understanding, progress, completion, satisfaction, and future use of knowledge. Questions for the approach category included the following: How will I approach the task? How hard will it be? How long will it take? Is there another way of doing it? Why am I doing the task? What will I get from it? and what will I make of the result?

Evaluation Notebook: Students evaluated their use of the questions from the Question-Asking Checklist for most of their science lessons during Phases 3 and 4 and recorded the results in this notebook. Data were collected from 15 different sources, including notebooks, classroom observations, audio and video recordings of lessons, interviews, questionnaires and teacher-made tests. The results showed that at the beginning of the study neither the 9th nor 11th graders were clear about their learning difficulties and they did not have strategies for overcoming them. During Phase 3, students became more aware about themselves as learners. During Phase 4, students improved in their ability to control their own learning.

Classroom Applications

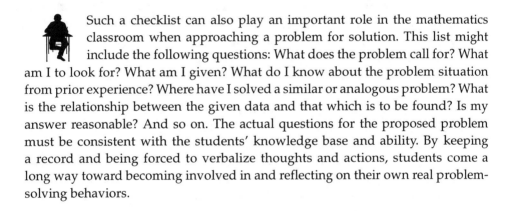 Such a checklist can also play an important role in the mathematics classroom when approaching a problem for solution. This list might include the following questions: What does the problem call for? What am I to look for? What am I given? What do I know about the problem situation from prior experience? Where have I solved a similar or analogous problem? What is the relationship between the given data and that which is to be found? Is my answer reasonable? And so on. The actual questions for the proposed problem must be consistent with the students' knowledge base and ability. By keeping a record and being forced to verbalize thoughts and actions, students come a long way toward becoming involved in and reflecting on their own real problem-solving behaviors.

Precautions and Possible Pitfalls

Teachers must be careful not to impose their checklist on the students. They must have students formulate their own list so that the items are meaningful and useful to the student. Students should have a feeling of ownership with the list, and questions should be adapted to the specific problem.

SOURCE

Baird, J. R., & White, R. T. (1984, April). *Improving learning through enhanced metacognition: A classroom study.* Paper presented at the annual meeting of the American Educational Research Association, New Orleans, LA.

THE TIP (1.10)

Examine your students' knowledge about mathematics and use this information to write challenging word problems that students will enjoy solving.

What the Research Says

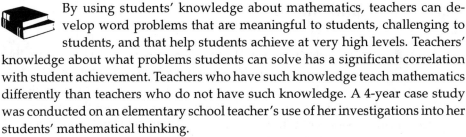

By using students' knowledge about mathematics, teachers can develop word problems that are meaningful to students, challenging to students, and that help students achieve at very high levels. Teachers' knowledge about what problems students can solve has a significant correlation with student achievement. Teachers who have such knowledge teach mathematics differently than teachers who do not have such knowledge. A 4-year case study was conducted on an elementary school teacher's use of her investigations into her students' mathematical thinking.

Instead of viewing her students as "blank slates," the teacher strongly believed in building on students' existing knowledge. She systematically investigated their mathematical thinking by interviewing them, by regularly asking them to explain how they solved problems, and by asking them to compare one problem solution to another. One way she used information about students' knowledge of mathematics was to develop a curriculum that primarily involved word problems. Although she wrote most of them, her students also successfully wrote word problems for themselves and each other to solve. They wrote different types of problems with varying levels of difficulty. Students were required to be able to solve all the problems they wrote. The teacher used students' activities and interests as the context of the problems she wrote. The results showed that students enjoyed writing problems and wanted to solve challenging problems with big numbers.

Classroom Applications

Compared with several decades ago, today, with the advent of the calculator and computer, the teacher has the freedom to use real world problems with "ugly numbers" that do not calculate to nicely rounded-off numbers, as was the case before such nifty calculating devices was readily available to all students. The question then is where can the teacher find the sources for problems that the students can easily relate to. For starters, the teacher should get to know her or his students as people. Find out what they like to do in their spare time—for example, what television shows they watch, what comics they read, what movies and video games they like. Building such interests into word problems can make them fun for students to solve. The teacher can also check local newspapers for sports events that might interest the youngsters, or for unusual sales being run by local merchants. The larger area (or national) newspapers can be consulted, for on practically every page there could be interesting ideas for mathematics applications. Sometimes the teacher will have to add some imagination or take the situation described one step further to speculate what may happen if . . . in a given situation. In any case, there is a wealth of information available for a teacher to discover ideas to create problems. For the teacher who does not see this as an activity that comes easily to him or her, it would be wise to form a small committee of teachers to work together on this effort. In a short time, teachers will get "the hang of it" and be able to continue independently. The results in student interest will be worth the effort expended.

Precautions and Possible Pitfalls

 The primary precaution here is to bear in mind that the topics are to be of interest to the students and not necessarily to the teacher. There are times when this "mix-up" will not be avoidable, but by being conscious of this possible pitfall, you will be a long way toward selecting appropriate examples.

SOURCE

Fennema, E., Franke, M. L., Carpenter, T. P., & Carey, D. A. (1993). Using children's mathematical knowledge in instruction. *American Educational Research Journal, 30*(3), 555-583.

THE TIP (1.11)

 Treat students in ways that reflect the belief that you have high expectations for their performance.

What the Research Says

Research has not supported the common belief that when teachers let students know that they have high expectations for their performance, a self-fulfilling prophesy will occur; however, research has shown that teacher expectations can influence student performance in another way. When teachers have high expectations for their students' performance, they tend to treat students differently than when teachers have low expectations for student performance. When teachers believe their students can perform at higher levels, they tend to give students more encouragement or more time to answer a question than when they have low expectations of student performance. As a result of this increased time and encouragement, students tend to achieve at higher levels.

Classroom Applications

It is not uncommon for a student to not feel too comfortable with absolute value inequalities, especially at first exposure. First, there is the problem of understanding (or conceptualizing) the notion of absolute value, then the student is required to understand how to express absolute value concepts in terms of inequalities. In short, it is not a terribly easy topic or concept for many students to master. To avoid student frustration, teachers should show high expectations of students as a form of motivation. Consequently, this is a particular topic where teacher patience and encouragement is very important. Patience and encouragement convey to the student that the teacher believes she or he can succeed. Praising performance for this topic may have a particular value because the topic can be formidable for some students.

Precautions and Possible Pitfalls

 Teachers should set realistic expectations, not expectations at a level so high that they are perceived as unattainable.

SOURCE

Good, T., & Brophy, J. (1984). *Looking in classrooms* (3rd edition). New York: Harper & Row.

THE TIP (1.12)

Use graphic representations or illustrations to enhance students' memory while they are listening to you. Abstract representations such as flow charts are more effective than colorful pictures!

What the Research Says

There are several types of supplementary materials that can help students remember what they learn while listening to a teacher. Some types of materials are better than others. One study compared the effect of graphic representations (flow charts with keywords) versus colorful pictures on students' memory. The study was conducted with 23 girls and 33 boys, aged 11-13 years. The entire sample was separated into four groups. In each group, students listened to a tape recording of textual material. The four groups included the following:

Group	Description
1	No graphic representation and no picture
2	Graphic representation (flow chart with key words from the text)
3	Colorful picture
4	Graphic representation and picture

After hearing the tape, students completed a questionnaire to check the effects of the different groups on students' memory. The results showed that students remembered more when they were given the graphic representations.

Classroom Applications

Pictures can inhibit memory of knowledge given auditorily. The complexity of a picture takes too much visual attention and stresses the capacity of intellectual processing. When students read a text, pictures can support the verbal information, because during reading a person can focus her or his attention either on the text or on the picture and the reader can move ahead at her or his own pace. Pictures can, however, interfere with listening. They can interrupt the logical flow of the words. Pictures and words only go together when the auditory information explains the picture. There are many types of graphic representations mathematics teachers can use. They can include

- flowcharts
- rough structural sketches
- continuums
- matrices
- Venn diagrams
- tree diagrams
- concept maps
- problem-solution charts

Graphic representations are characterized by being quickly understood; they provide a structure for integrating new information, and they are schematized sketches instead of colorful pictures.

Example 1: Repetition of characteristics of triangles

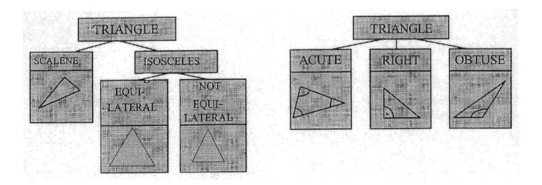

Precautions and Possible Pitfalls

 The following illustration (Example 2) demonstrates that not every graphic representation aids learning and memory. The representation in Example 2 draws too much attention away from what students will be listening to because it is too complex. It combines several characteristic classifications into one representation. That is why it is recommended to construct a graphic representation as simply as possible if students are to see it while they are listening. A complex representation such as the one in Example 2 may be useful for students when they are not listening to a lesson.

Example 2:

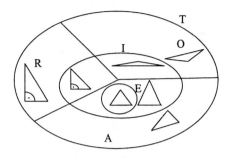

T: Set of all triangles

A: Set of all acute triangles

O: Set of all obtuse triangles

R: Set of all right triangles

I: Set of all isosceles triangles

E: Set of all equilateral triangles

SOURCE

Imhof, M., Echtrernach, B., Huber, S., & Knorr, S. (1996). Hören und Sehen: Behaltensrelavante Effekte von Illustrationen beim Zuhören [Ear and eye: Retention of effects of illustrations in listening tasks]. *Unterrichtswissenschaft Zeitschrift für Lernforschung, 24*(4), 329-342.

THE TIP (1.13)

 Make sure to pause for at least 4 seconds after listening to a student's communication, before responding.

What the Research Says

Extensive research for over 20 years has compared extended pauses or "wait time" to normal pauses after a student's communication. Normal pauses average around one second. In a study of mathematics classes of 20 teachers covering the topic of probability reasoning, one group of teachers was taught to use extended pauses after listening to a student's communication while the other group used their normal pauses. When teachers paused for at least 4 seconds after listening to a student's communication before giving a response, middle school students had higher achievement in mathematics, and were more likely to give thoughtful, detailed responses than those when teachers' responses came immediately after students spoke.

Classroom Applications

Instead of responding immediately to the student's communication, teachers should pause at least 4 seconds after a student initiates a communication, such as an answer, question, or comment. This extended pause has the following benefits: (a) it allows students to think of a greater number of ideas, (b) it leads to students thinking of more details about their ideas, (c) it gives more of an opportunity for other students to think about what the student communicating said, so another student can respond to the student's communication instead of the teacher, (d) it promotes higher levels of achievement in mathematics, and (e) it shows students, through teacher modeling, that it is appropriate to take time for reflection—to think about an answer before speaking.

Precautions and Possible Pitfalls

1. Teachers often respond quickly to students' questions and other communications. This rapid follow-up stifles higher-level thinking, the elaboration of ideas, and cuts students off who were about to elaborate on their ideas.

2. This tip sounds deceptively simple, but research shows it is hard for teachers to change their normal pausing habit and maintain a 4-second pause before answering students.

3. The more complex the communication, the longer the pause should be.

SOURCES

Tobin, K. (1986). Effects of teacher wait time on discourse characteristics in mathematics and language arts classes. *American Educational Research Journal, 23*(2), 191-200.

Tobin, K. (1987). The role of wait time in higher cognitive-level learning. *Review of Educational Research, 57*(1), 69-95.

THE TIP (1.14)

 When doing inquiry lessons, give students clearly written materials to guide the inquiry process.

What the Research Says

Research on the inquiry-based computer program Geometric Supposers was conducted in 23 high school geometry classes. This program uses teacher-posed inquiry problems. The researchers specifically designed the materials so they would clearly communicate to the students what the particular problem is and what appropriate inquiry activities are expected. Evidence was collected from six sources: classroom observations, student interviews, students' work on the Supposers program, teacher interviews, teacher reflections, and minutes from monthly teachers' meetings. The results showed that (a) clearly written materials mean students will understand what work needs to be done, (b) they help students organize their work, (c) using charts and tables that tell students which measurements to make and giving step-by-step instructions was ineffective because it limited their inquiry. These findings led the researchers to conclude that how inquiry materials are written affects students' success in inquiry.

Classroom Applications

 Teachers should prepare clearly written materials for students— making sure to leave an opportunity for students to conduct an inquiry. Three strategies for writing clear materials include the following:

1. State the goal of the problem at the top of the page.
2. Provide explicit instructions on the processes to use when solving the problem so students know how to engage in inquiry; do not provide so much structure that it stifles student inquiry so that students only collect data or follow directions without understanding what they are doing.
3. After students understand how diagrams can be used as models, use diagrams to simplify written instructions.

Sample goal statement: Task: To develop a procedure that enables you to reproduce or reconstruct the following figure.

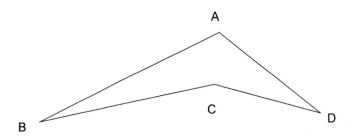

Sample process instructions: Procedure:

Make a drawing similar to this figure.

Collect data.

Describe below the procedures for reproducing this figure.

State your conjectures.

Precautions and Possible Pitfalls

 Unclearly written materials prevent students from successful inquiry. When creating inquiry problems for students, teachers should consider three issues before writing the problem statement and three issues while writing it. The three issues to consider before writing the problem statement include the kind of problem, its scope, and the students' background or ability. Three issues to consider while writing the problem statement include stating the goal of the problem, describing any constructions in the problem, and instructions for inquiry processes students are expected to use.

SOURCE

Yerushalmy, M., Chazan, D., & Gordon, M. (1990). Mathematical problem posing: Implications for facilitating student inquiry in classrooms. *Instructional Science, 19,* 219-245.

THE TIP (1.15)

 To make inquiry lessons more effective, pose structured inquiry problems to students.

What the Research Says

Research on the inquiry-based computer program Geometric Supposers was conducted in 23 high school geometry classes. This program uses teacher-posed inquiry problems. These problems are open-ended and can be approached in many ways. They have many solutions and are related to the teacher's agenda. They are worthwhile problems to explore; they resemble those that an expert would work on. They are not simple, neat little exercises with a single right answer.

Problems were constructed for each of three instructional roles: applying previously learned concepts, helping students become familiar with relationships in a construction, and discovering theorems. Some problems were more structured and gave students more directions than other problems. The amount of structure and directions depended on the type of instructional role the teacher had in mind for the problem. Evidence was collected from six sources: classroom observations, student interviews, student work on the Supposers program, teacher interviews, teacher reflections, and minutes from monthly teachers' meetings. The results showed that well-designed problems have the following benefits: they make the inquiry approach clearer; they can define the relationship between the content of the curriculum and the use of the computer software, and affect the success of the problems. The results showed that the success of problems depended on their instructional role.

Classroom Applications

An example to illustrate how inquiry may be used in the high school mathematics classroom could involve having students draw any irregularly shaped quadrilateral. After locating the midpoints of each of the four sides, students should be asked to join these midpoints consecutively. The resulting figure will be a parallelogram (always!). They now can begin their inquiry work by trying to determine under which circumstances various types of parallelograms appear. Structure the problem so that students have to justify (or prove) why this is so. You can also structure the problem to extend their inquiry further to other polygons (beyond the quadrilateral) and/or to select other points besides the midpoints of the sides. There are many extensions of this original configuration that teachers can build into the structure to guide students to undertake further inquiry. The Geometer's Sketchpad (Key Curriculum Press) software program can be particularly useful here.

Precautions and Possible Pitfalls

 Be careful not to provide too much structure or too little structure. Too much structure will prevent meaningful inquiry and lead to boredom. Too little structure will make students confused and frustrated and can create anxiety.

SOURCE

Yerushalmy, M., Chazan, D., & Gordon, M. (1990). Mathematical problem posing: Implications for facilitating student inquiry in classrooms. *Instructional Science, 19*, 219-245.

THE TIP (1.16)

 Use practical applications to help students understand an abstraction and to promote long-term memory.

What the Research Says

 A study, involving three ninth-grade classes (83 students) and three teachers, examined using a different sequence of presentation when teaching new, abstract information. Instead of focusing on learning a new abstract concept through the traditional procedure of explaining the concept, a study experimented with beginning instruction with practical applications of the concept. The three classes were separated into two experimental classes (A and B) and one control class (C). The researchers evaluated the accuracy of students' knowledge (precision), students' ability to recall or recognize the information (availability), and long-term memory (after 3 months) of what was learned (durability). The results showed that the experimental classes performed better than the control class on all three measures. Students in the experimental classes were also better able to understand the phenomena observed, and to make, explain, and remember connections between ideas than students in the control class.

Classroom Applications

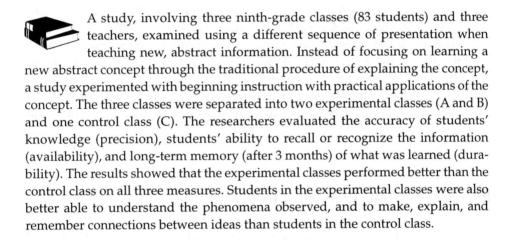

1. Demonstrate an experiment that shows a certain effect under specific conditions.
2. Give practical examples for the viewed phenomenon and ask students to describe the principles. Students can do this in groups.

This procedure is similar to the well-known Learning Cycle Model, which is based on Piagetian theory and involves a constructivist approach to teaching. It is intended to help students progress from concrete to abstract thinking about content (i.e., from concrete to formal operations). A learning cycle comprises three stages: exploration, concept introduction/development, and application.

Stage 1: Exploration

Exploration involves students getting hands-on experience working with the content to be focused on during the learning cycle. The teacher provides students with materials and guides students' experience with them. For example, the teacher may give a group of students a bag of candy and ask them to give each student in the group the same amount of candy.

Stage 2: Concept Introduction
     Students' experiences from their exploration are used to introduce basic concepts to be learned, such as division, fractions, and percentages.

Stage 3: Application
     The application phase of the learning cycle "challenges" students to generalize the concepts of the lesson to other situations. They solve new problems by applying what they learned during Stages 1 and 2. Ideally, the teacher will assign tasks or problems that relate to students' everyday lives. For example, for homework the students might have to ask family members to share equally in washing the dishes after dinner and explain how they made sure everyone in the family had the same amount of dishes to wash using the concepts focused on in class.
     Students' thinking is expected to have progressed from concrete thinking about the concepts to be learned to being able to deal with this content on a formal, abstract level.

Precautions and Possible Pitfalls

 If you plan the period for such practical application, allow more time than usual. Students who normally do not actively participate in class or who have difficulties in mathematics may become more actively involved in this type of learning activity than they do with traditional instruction. If you find their ideas are incorrect, carefully and gently give them corrective feedback so you don't discourage their continued active involvement.

SOURCES

Nickerson, R. S., Perkins, D. N., & Smith, E. E. (1985). *The teaching of thinking.* Hillsdale, NJ: Lawrence Erlbaum.
Stange, E.-M. (1985). Zur Erhöhung der geistigen Aktivität der Schüler im Physikunterricht durch Beachtung lernpsychologischer Erkenntnisse— dargestellt am Beispiel der Stoffeinheit "Elektromagnetische Induktion" Klasse 9 [Increasing of student's intellectual activity by consideration of aspects of the psychology of learning—as seen through the topic "electromagnetic induction" in Grade 9]. *Pädagogische Forschung, 26*(4), 42-51.

THE TIP (1.17)

Systematically incorporate review into your instructional plans, especially before beginning a new topic.

What the Research Says

Research on the types and timing of review in mathematics teaching shows that daily review of homework assignments is not enough. Review should be systematically integrated into lesson plans, especially before beginning a new topic. Such reviews help the teacher to plan so that students have the prerequisite knowledge and skills needed to successfully learn new material. Studies have shown that in addition to helping teachers plan instruction, review helps students (a) consolidate what they have learned, (b) summarize the main ideas, (c) develop generalizations, (d) develop a more comprehensive view of the topics, (e) get a "big picture" of how ideas fit together, and (f) feel confident that they are ready to move on to a new topic. Research on the timing of review suggests it is more effective when it is interspersed throughout the curriculum instead of being concentrated at one period of time. Research has been conducted on a range of review techniques. Studies show that student-generated outlines force students to organize ideas and structure the relationships between them. Such outlines have been found to enhance the recall of mathematical ideas. Review questions have been found to aid memory by increasing understanding. Questions can be word or calculation based. Research indicates that word-type questions require students to comprehend concepts and rules well enough to apply them to new situations. In contrast, calculation-type questions generally require understanding only a small range of concepts and rules, and often only involve rote learning.

Classroom Applications

Before beginning a new topic, teachers should review to identify which prerequisite knowledge and skills students have acquired, which should be taught again for reinforcement, and which are not yet known. When conducting a review, the teacher should include a broad range of content, from simple skills and concepts to the most difficult skills and concepts. There are several different types of review used in mathematics, including outlines, questions, homework, and tests.

To simply ask students if they remember a certain topic is insufficient in determining the students' readiness for a new topic. For example, when embarking on an algebraically "heavy" topic in the midst of the geometry course, it would be wise to select the main skill that will be required of the students in that unit and give them a short, informal quiz on the topic. For example, if the Pythagorean Theorem is to be studied, some review of topics such as radicals would be appropriate.

You might also give students a series of questions that should be done at home. Those would be designed to require simple ideas from the past. Students will then have a "pressure-free" opportunity to exhibit their knowledge, after conducting a private review.

Precautions and Possible Pitfalls

 When embarking on a review of things previously taught, avoid being dissuaded by students who are quick to tell the teacher "we already had this stuff." They may have been taught it, but did they learn this material? This is what must be ascertained by the teacher. One effective way of doing this is by having students demonstrate and explain to the teacher what they know about the material to be reviewed rather than boring the students by repeating what they have been shown or told before.

SOURCE

Suydam, M. N. (1984). *The role of review in mathematics instruction* (ERIC/SMEAC Mathematics Digest No. 2. ED260891). Columbus, OH: ERIC Clearinghouse for Science, Mathematics, and Environmental Education.

THE TIP (1.18)

 Make realistic time estimates when planning your lessons.

What the Research Says

Teachers need to have excellent time management skills for students to learn effectively. It is sometimes said that "time + energy = learning." Sometimes teachers confuse time allocated for instruction with time students are actually engaged in learning. The concept of engaged time is often referred to as "time-on-task." Teachers often fail to take into account the time they end up devoting to managing student behavior and managing classroom activities. Teachers need to take this distinction between allocated and engaged time into account when estimating how much time it will take for students to learn a particular set of material. It's the time students actually spend learning that is the key to the amount of achievement.

Classroom Applications

Suppose you are planning a lesson on the introduction to the Law of Sines. You would like to develop or derive the Law and you would like to have ample time to apply the Law to "practical" examples as well as the drill that typically follows the introduction of the Law. To fit this into a normal 50-minute lesson, you might either relegate a more serious inspection of the derivation to a homework assignment and simply introduce the Law of Sines and its applications to the triangle, or you may search for a concise derivation of the Law of Sines such as the following:

Consider the circumcircle of $\triangle$ ABC with diameter $\overline{AD}$.

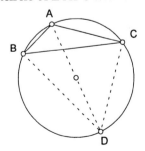

$$\text{Diameter } AD = \frac{AC}{\sin\angle ADC} = \frac{AC}{\sin\angle ABC}$$

(Since $\angle ADC$ and $\angle ABC$ are inscribed in the same arc.)

Similarly,

$$\text{Diameter } AD = \frac{AB}{\sin\angle ADB} = \frac{AB}{\sin\angle ACB}. \text{ Therefore, } \frac{AC}{\sin\angle ABC} = \frac{AB}{\sin\angle ACB},$$

which can then be followed in a similar way to the third part of the Law of Sines. This very concise proof will allow the teacher ample time to do a complete lesson on a topic that would otherwise require more than one lesson to introduce. In other words, it is wise for a teacher in planning a lesson and trying to ensure that there is enough time to do the lesson to also search for alternative methods that might be more concise and allow for a more streamlined lesson. The above plan requires that teachers be aware of unexpected interuptions that may interfere with allocated time.

Precautions and Possible Pitfalls

 Be sure to plan time in your "clever" lesson time for your students to "digest" the cleverness of proofs or demonstrations that may not be in the textbook. This will ensure that they have time to take complete notes of the development you are doing in the lesson, so that review at home is then possible.

SOURCE

Brophy, J. (1988). Research linking teacher behavior to student achievement: Potential implications for instruction of Chapter 1 students. *Educational Psychologist, 23,* 235-286.

THE TIP (1.19)

 Questions can have many functions in the classroom.

What the Research Says

 Research was conducted to investigate what questions teachers asked and why they asked them. Thirty-six high school teachers from five schools, representing all subject areas, participated in the study. They were asked to give examples of the questions they asked, to explain how they used them, and to tell to whom the questions were addressed. In general, the results showed that teachers ask questions to obtain information, to maintain control, and to test knowledge. Many specific functions of classroom questions were identified. These functions are listed next.

Classroom Applications

 The following is a list of functions classroom questions can serve:

1. To stimulate curiosity or interest about a topic
2. To concentrate attention on a specific concept or issue
3. To actively involve students in learning
4. To structure a task for maximal learning
5. To identify specific problems interfering with students' learning
6. To let a group of students know that their active involvement in the lesson was expected, and that each person's contribution to the group was important
7. To give students an opportunity to reflect on information and integrate it with what they already know
8. To develop students' thinking skills
9. To stimulate discussions in which students and the teacher develop and reflect on ideas, thereby enabling students to learn from others
10. To show genuine interest in students' ideas and feelings

Precautions and Possible Pitfalls

There is a variety of the types of questions to avoid in order to make classroom questions maximally effective. There are, however, certain techniques that also merit attention. For example, to maintain student interest in one another's responses, teachers should avoid repeating a student's response even if it was inaudible to the others. Have students who don't speak loudly repeat their response louder for others to hear. After a while, students will become so annoyed with the teacher's request to speak more loudly, they will begin to do it automatically and students will adopt the habit of listening to each other, realizing that the teacher will not repeat the response of a student. Another technique in asking questions properly is to avoid rephrasing a teacher's question for fear that it's original rendition may have been unclear (unless students indicate they are unclear). Surprisingly, there is usually more clarity to the original question, while unsolicited rephrasing might actually confuse those who understood the first version and now have trouble understanding the second version, thereby causing total confusion.

For additional pitfalls in questions see the chapter on Classroom Questioning in *Teaching Secondary School Mathematics: Techniques and Enrichment Units* by A. S. Posamentier and J. Stepelman (Merrill/Prentice Hall, 1998.

SOURCE

Brown, G. A., & Edmondson, R. (1984). Asking questions. In E. C. Wragg (Ed.), *Classroom teaching skills* (pp. 97–120). New York: Nichols.

THE TIP (1.20)

 Teachers can help students learn to ask better questions.

What the Research Says

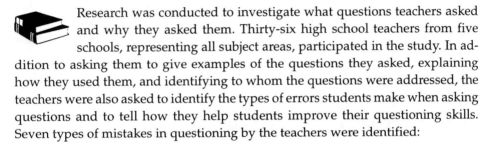 Research was conducted to investigate what questions teachers asked and why they asked them. Thirty-six high school teachers from five schools, representing all subject areas, participated in the study. In addition to asking them to give examples of the questions they asked, explaining how they used them, and identifying to whom the questions were addressed, the teachers were also asked to identify the types of errors students make when asking questions and to tell how they help students improve their questioning skills. Seven types of mistakes in questioning by the teachers were identified:

1. *Delivery:* Questions that were unclear; too fast, too slow, too quiet, or too loud; and not having eye contact with students while questioning

2. *Structure:* Questions with unclear demands, such as using unclear vocabulary, and making questions too long or too complex

3. *Target:* Questions directed inappropriately to either an individual, a group, or the whole class

4. *Background:* Questions that were not put in the proper context of the lesson or problems with questioning sequences

5. *Handling answers:* Not allowing enough time for students to answer questions or accepting only answers that were expected

6. *Discipline and management:* Avoiding students all calling out answers at the same time and making sure all students can hear both the questions and the answers

7. *Level:* Asking questions that are too hard or too easy for the specific students targeted

Teachers made several suggestions for helping students ask better questions. They recommended providing students with models of good questions for students to observe, discussing effective questioning strategies, giving students opportunities to practice questioning, and providing students with feedback on their questioning.

Classroom Applications

Making students aware of what a proper question is, may, in the long run, make them better learners and give them the ability to pose better questions. Teachers should demonstrate and discuss the characteristics of effective and ineffective questions. It may prove fruitful to have students critique each other's questions, either in pairs or in a group. Alternatively, give a list of student-generated questions to students and have them critique them as a homework assignment. There is a fair amount of information available about proper questioning techniques. Students need to know what makes effective classroom questioning as well as what things could make the questions counterproductive. A good source on this topic would be *Teaching Secondary School Mathematics: Techniques and Enrichment Units* by A. S. Posamentier and J. Stepelman (Merrill/Prentice Hall, 1998).

Precautions and Possible Pitfalls

Given peer pressures, students critiquing each others' questions may be a bit of a challenge for the teacher. Avoid embarrassing students for asking ineffective questions by calling attention to them in a whole-class setting. Teachers who attempt this suggestion for implementation must be aware that this is meant to be an enhancement for the instructional program and not a deterrent. If one technique doesn't seem to work with a particular class, it ought to be replaced with a more effective approach.

SOURCE

Brown, G. A., & Edmondson, R. (1984). Asking questions. In E. C. Wragg (Ed.), *Classroom teaching skills* (pp. 97–120). New York: Nichols.

THE TIP (1.21)

   Questions can be asked in a variety of sequences.

What the Research Says

Investigating what questions teachers asked and why they asked them was the focus of research conducted among 36 high school teachers from 5 schools, representing all subject areas. They were asked to give examples of the questions they asked, to explain how they used them, and to tell to whom the questions were addressed. In addition, teachers were asked to give examples of questioning sequences they used and the context in which these sequences were used.

Eight types of sequences emerged from the results:

1. *Extending:* A chain of questions on the same topic and of the same type

2. *Extending and lifting:* First the questions ask for the same types of examples, then there is a change to a different type of question, at a higher level

3. *Funneling:* Start with open questions and then get progressively narrower

4. *Sowing and reaping:* First a problem is posed and open questions are asked. Then questions become more specific. Finally, the original problem is restated

5. *Step-by-step up:* Systematically move from recall to problem solving, evaluation, or open-ended questions

6. *Step-by-step down:* Systematically move from problem solving to direct recall

7. *Nose-dive:* Start with problem solving or evaluation questions and then move directly to direct recall

8. *Random walk:* No clear pattern of questioning content or type

Classroom Applications

 Practice with the above forms of questioning sequences by considering one strategy at a time. Students can be guided nicely through mathematical proofs using an effective line of questioning; therefore, this may be just the right place to try these "skills." It should be noted that the questioning in doing proofs (most notably seen in the geometry course) can further be channeled to take into account the backwards strategy that should be used for all deductive proofs no matter how simple. Students should be guided to begin at the end (the desired conclusion) and then work backwards asking a variety of different types of questions until the given information is reached.

Precautions and Possible Pitfalls

 Some of the questioning sequences listed are better than others. Don't let students fall into the trap of thinking that all questions and questioning sequences are of equal value. Help them critically evaluate the value of each question and question sequence and consider situations in which each would and would not be desirable.

SOURCE

Brown, G. A., & Edmondson, R. (1984). Asking questions. In E. C. Wragg (Ed.), *Classroom teaching skills* (pp. 97–120). New York: Nichols.

THE TIP (1.22)

 Use a variety of strategies to encourage students to ask questions about difficult assignments.

What the Research Says

 Several approaches have been identified that can help to overcome students' reluctance to ask questions:

1. Avoid giving students the impression that the reasons for the difficulties are their own.

2. In cases in which students have difficulties with problems, do not indicate that the problem was simple.

3. Give external reasons for students' difficulties.

Research has shown that people can handle their neediness better if they can attribute the reasons for their neediness to external causes. One study investigated asking questions as a kind of neediness. Participants were 24 girls and 24 boys, with a mean age of 14 years.

Students were confronted with the following situation. They got an unformatted text that included typing mistakes. Students had to format the text according to a given pattern.

The results showed the following:

- Students showed the most willingness to ask questions when they could hold external circumstances responsible for their neediness.
- Students' willingness to ask questions decreased when they had the impression that the person they asked blamed them for the difficulty. In this case, if the student asked a question, it would hurt their self-esteem.
- Students avoided asking questions if the person they asked indicated the task was simple.

Classroom Applications

Teachers should explicitly and implicitly encourage students to ask questions. Asking questions is not easy for students in many cases. Sometimes, even simple questions require both a minimum of knowledge/understanding and courage. Teachers should help students feel that there are no such things as silly questions, although teachers sometimes give silly answers! Asking questions is one of the most valuable skills a person can develop. Teachers can say that "silly" questions are often the very best questions! Teachers should:

- Give positive comments about students' questions.
  Examples:

  > "Good question!"

  > "Instead of getting grades for good answers, you should get grades for good questions!"

  > "Your questions shows that you've thought about this a lot."

  > "Very interesting question!"

- Encourage students to ask questions by emphasizing the difficulties of the task or of the working conditions.
  Examples:

  > "Some aspects of this problem are hidden. Consequently, you might have some difficulties."

  > "Asking questions in public can often be difficult . . . but try nonetheless! It will get easier with practice."

- If students begin to attribute difficulties to their own lack of ability, try to direct their attention to the external difficulties.
  Examples:

  > "Make sure you pay careful attention to the difficult parts of this problem."

  > "This is a new type of problem. We haven't discussed it yet."

  > "Do not rush your thought process, some of the smartest people think slowly."

- Do not express doubt about students' capabilities or skills.
  Negative examples:

  > "I already answered that question three times."

  > "Listen carefully to what I say!"

Positive examples:

> "When students ask me a question a third time, that tells me that something may be wrong with my explanation."

> "Sometimes I may explain things too quickly; you must let me know."

Precautions and Possible Pitfalls

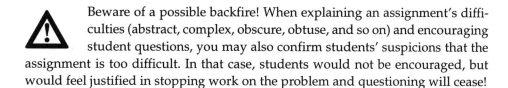 Beware of a possible backfire! When explaining an assignment's difficulties (abstract, complex, obscure, obtuse, and so on) and encouraging student questions, you may also confirm students' suspicions that the assignment is too difficult. In that case, students would not be encouraged, but would feel justified in stopping work on the problem and questioning will cease!

SOURCE

Fuhrer, U. (1994). Fragehemmungen bei Schülerinnen und Schülern: Eine attributierungstheoretische Erklärung [Pupils' inhibition to ask questions: An attributional analysis]. *Zeitschrift für Pädagogische Psychologie, 8,* 103-109.

THE TIP (1.23)

 Teach students to ask themselves questions about the problems/tasks they are working on.

What the Research Says

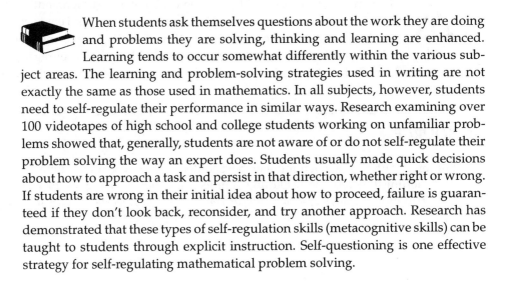 When students ask themselves questions about the work they are doing and problems they are solving, thinking and learning are enhanced. Learning tends to occur somewhat differently within the various subject areas. The learning and problem-solving strategies used in writing are not exactly the same as those used in mathematics. In all subjects, however, students need to self-regulate their performance in similar ways. Research examining over 100 videotapes of high school and college students working on unfamiliar problems showed that, generally, students are not aware of or do not self-regulate their problem solving the way an expert does. Students usually made quick decisions about how to approach a task and persist in that direction, whether right or wrong. If students are wrong in their initial idea about how to proceed, failure is guaranteed if they don't look back, reconsider, and try another approach. Research has demonstrated that these types of self-regulation skills (metacognitive skills) can be taught to students through explicit instruction. Self-questioning is one effective strategy for self-regulating mathematical problem solving.

Classroom Applications

Teach students to ask themselves questions before, during, and after they solve problems or work on other tasks. Their questions should be formulated so they specifically focus on the problem or task at hand. Examples include the following: What technique did I use to solve a similar problem in the past? How do I find the derivative? What is the problem asking for? What information am I given? Students should also ask themselves general questions designed to self-regulate their performance, such as the following: Is there anything I don't understand? Am I headed in the right direction? Is there any information given in the problem that is not immediately obvious? Have I made any careless mistakes? In mathematics, the reasonableness of the answer obtained is often not considered. Students believe that mathematics problems are contrived; therefore, the solutions do not really apply to the real world. This self-regulating experience should be extended to this aspect of self-checking by considering not only the procedure used, but also the meaningfulness of the answer arrived at.

Precautions and Possible Pitfalls

Questions generated by the students themselves are more effective than questions provided to them by the teacher. Although student questions are often unpolished and may even sound inaccurate, students understand them and may resent having the questions sharpened by the teacher. Allow students grammatical and content freedom in their private self-questioning activity, or else you may spoil the genuineness of the experience with largely irrelevant, extraneous factors, however well intentioned they may be.

SOURCE

Schoenfeld, A. (1989). Teaching mathematical thinking and problem solving. In L. B. Resnick & L. E. Klopfer (Eds.), *Toward the thinking curriculum: Current cognitive research* (pp. 83-103). Alexandria, VA: Association for Supervision and Curriculum Development.

THE TIP (1.24)

 Teach students to ask themselves questions about what they already know about a problem or task they are working on.

What the Research Says

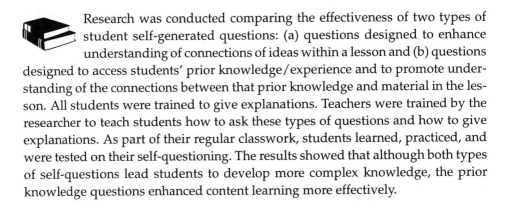 Research was conducted comparing the effectiveness of two types of student self-generated questions: (a) questions designed to enhance understanding of connections of ideas within a lesson and (b) questions designed to access students' prior knowledge/experience and to promote understanding of the connections between that prior knowledge and material in the lesson. All students were trained to give explanations. Teachers were trained by the researcher to teach students how to ask these types of questions and how to give explanations. As part of their regular classwork, students learned, practiced, and were tested on their self-questioning. The results showed that although both types of self-questions lead students to develop more complex knowledge, the prior knowledge questions enhanced content learning more effectively.

Classroom Applications

Teach students to question themselves about what they already know about a topic and how this knowledge relates to the current problem/ situation. For example, "What do I know about this type of problem?" "How have I solved problems like this before?" Then teach them to ask themselves how this information applies to the current problem or situation. For example, "How can I use that approach in this situation?"

Student-generated self-questions are very effective thinking and learning tools. These self-questions need to be formulated for the specific problem or task the student is working on. Student-generated questions are superior to teacher-generated questions that are given to students to use. Not all self-questions are equally valuable. When doing problem solving in a mathematics course, there are many times when students should ask themselves questions. This form of silent questioning is an excellent way of guiding oneself through the solution of a problem. This sort of self-questioning replaces the typical teacher questioning and begins to develop a problem-solving independence in the student. Not only do crazy people talk to themselves, people solving a mathematics problem do so, as well!

Precautions and Possible Pitfalls

 Be alert to the possibility that some of the students' prior knowledge may be somewhat faulty.

SOURCE

King, A. (1994). Guiding knowledge construction in the classroom: Effects of teaching children how to question and how to explain. *American Educational Research Journal, 31*(2), 338-368.

THE TIP (1.25)

 Teachers should be tactical in their use of questions.

What the Research Says

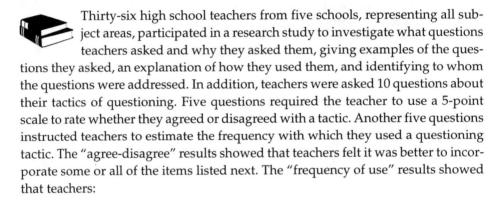 Thirty-six high school teachers from five schools, representing all subject areas, participated in a research study to investigate what questions teachers asked and why they asked them, giving examples of the questions they asked, an explanation of how they used them, and identifying to whom the questions were addressed. In addition, teachers were asked 10 questions about their tactics of questioning. Five questions required the teacher to use a 5-point scale to rate whether they agreed or disagreed with a tactic. Another five questions instructed teachers to estimate the frequency with which they used a questioning tactic. The "agree-disagree" results showed that teachers felt it was better to incorporate some or all of the items listed next. The "frequency of use" results showed that teachers:

1. address questions to the whole class about half of the time;

2. call on students by name about half of the time;

3. praise students for correctly answering a question frequently, but not always;

4. occasionally get students to ask each other questions; and

5. occasionally go all the way around the class getting each student to answer a question.

Classroom Applications

 The following are just a few suggestions for questioning tactics:

1. Select a student to answer a question after the question has been asked.

2. Get another student to correct a student's incorrect answer instead of the teacher making the correction (students will begin to listen to each other's responses more carefully if they know that the teacher will not repeat a student's response).

3. Rephrase a question if the class doesn't understand it (after a reasonable waiting period). Too many and too frequently rephrased questions can cause further confusion.

4. Orally discuss important questions rather than having students write the answers.

5. Audio or videotape yourself while teaching to observe and evaluate you own questioning tactics; then, develop a plan to improve your questioning tactics.

Far more space would be required here to treat this topic properly. We refer the interested reader to *Teaching Secondary School Mathematics: Techniques and Enrichment Units* by A. S. Posamentier and J. Stepelman (Merrill/Prentice Hall, 1998) for a more in-depth treatment of the topic.

Precautions and Possible Pitfalls

 Much of this is dependent on teacher sensitivity. Remember, this is supposed to be a lesson-enhancing device. Do not get so hung up thinking about the teaching technique that it detracts from the lesson itself. Constant monitoring, not only of test results, but also an objective observation of student behavior, would be appropriate.

SOURCE

Brown, G. A., & Edmondson, R. (1984). Asking questions. In E. C. Wragg (Ed.), *Classroom teaching skills* (pp. 97–120). New York: Nichols.

THE TIP (1.26)

 Make a lesson more stimulating and interesting by varying the types of questions you ask students.

What the Research Says

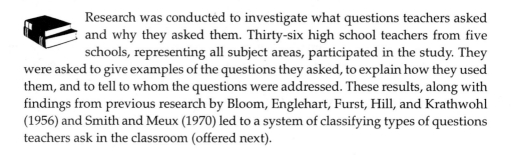 Research was conducted to investigate what questions teachers asked and why they asked them. Thirty-six high school teachers from five schools, representing all subject areas, participated in the study. They were asked to give examples of the questions they asked, to explain how they used them, and to tell to whom the questions were addressed. These results, along with findings from previous research by Bloom, Englehart, Furst, Hill, and Krathwohl (1956) and Smith and Meux (1970) led to a system of classifying types of questions teachers ask in the classroom (offered next).

Classroom Applications

There are many types of questions to use as well as many to avoid. Many of the nondrill topics in mathematics require understanding. When a topic that requires thought and deduction is being considered, it is wise to ask lots of questions. Each question should be succinct and structured in such a way to lead the students through a mathematical development or argument. One example is the sort of questioning that a teacher might use when guiding a student through a geometry proof. Here the questioning can take the form of factual questions or questions that have no definite answer, but require a judgment to be made. Following is the list mentioned earlier.

Cognitive questions

1. Recall data, task procedures, values, or knowledge. This category includes naming, classifying, reading out loud, providing known definitions, and observing.

2. Make simple deductions usually based on data that have been provided. This category includes comparing, giving simple descriptions and interpretations, and giving examples of principles.

3. Give reasons, hypotheses, causes, or motives that were not taught in the lesson.

4. Solve problems, using sequences of reasoning.

5. Evaluate one's own work, a topic, or a set of values.

Speculative, affective, and management questions

1. Make speculations, intuitive guesses, creative ideas, or approaches and open-ended questions (which have more than one right answer and permit a wide range of responses).

2. Encourage expressions of empathy and feelings.

3. Manage individuals, groups, or the entire class. This category includes checking that students understand a task, seeking compliance, controlling a situation, and directing students' attention.

Precautions and Possible Pitfalls

Even good questions can lose their value if they are overused. Avoid asking ambiguous questions and questions requiring only one-word answers, such as yes/no questions. To focus on a questioning style as indicated previously, but without proper concern to the subject matter, would be a misuse of this tip.

SOURCES

Bloom, B. S., Englehart, M. D., Furst, E. J., Hill, W. H., & Krathwohl, D. R. (1956). *Taxonomy of educational objectives, handbook 1—Cognitive domain.* New York: David McKay.

Brown, G. A., & Edmondson, R. (1984). Asking questions. In E. C. Wragg (Ed.), *Classroom teaching skills* (pp. 97–120). New York: Nichols.

Smith, B., & Meux, M. (1970). *A study of the logic of teaching.* Chicago: University of Illinois Press.

THE TIP (1.27)

 Consider whether a student's learning weakness might involve a deficiency in auditory perception.

What the Research Says

Sometimes learning difficulties are due to physical abnormalities rather than simply basic skill deficiencies. To find out possible causes of learning problems, research was conducted to investigate whether students' problems could be explained by disorders in auditory perception. The Mottier-Test was administered to 104 students who were identified as having learning problems and who had been treated by psychologists because of their learning problems.

The design of the test was as follows: The students had to listen to and repeat a total of 30 nonsense words (words without a real sense). Words on the list became progressively longer and more complex. The results of the experiment revealed that all the students, whether they had repeated a grade or not, had problems in auditory perception.

Classroom Applications

In addition to other possible causes, sometimes learning difficulties can signal deeper problems in auditory perception. Students who cannot understand what they hear will have problems comprehending information and directions given by the teacher. They will also be unable to follow comments of other students. Hence, teachers should have some background knowledge in auditory perception problems to recognize the symptoms and assist in the remediation process. To determine whether students might have difficulties in auditory perception that are affecting their learning, teachers can use a test such as the Mottier-Test.

Precautions and Possible Pitfalls

It is not necessary to specifically use the Mottier-Test to diagnose an auditory perception problem. Teachers can construct their own tests, quite simply, with the same effects. Although a teacher-constructed test will not be recognized as a valid test, it can provide teachers with a sign whether or not follow-up on auditory perception is worthwhile. Consideration should be given to the possibility of other causes, such as a temporary deficiency in a student's concentration or difficulty in spelling. It is recommended that the test be administered two or three times to check whether the results reflect a serious problem or a chance occurrence. To determine if either problems in auditory perception or in spelling produced the learning problems, contact a language teacher for his or her experiences with the student concerned.

SOURCE

Wagner, H. (1990). Auditive Merkfähigkeit bei Schülern: Eine Studie zum Mottier-Test [Auditory memory in school-age children: A study about the Mottier-Test]. *Psychologie in Erziehung und Unterricht, 37,* 33-37.

THE TIP (1.28)

Some students do not think that they have control over their academic successes and failures. Help these students recognize that they do have some control.

What the Research Says

Research has demonstrated that students differ in their perceptions of control over their successes and failures. Some students externalize responsibility (externalizers) whereas other students internalize this responsibility (internalizers). Externalizers assume powerful other people, such as teachers and parents, are responsible for their performance. Externalizers often also assume that chance plays an important role in their destiny. Internalizers perceive that they have control over their own destiny and are responsible for their own performance.

A study was conducted with 198 male and female college students; some were externalizers and some were internalizers. Before hearing a lecture, a group of internalizers and externalizers was shown an 8-minute color videotape of a psychology professor who told about his freshman year in college. He kept failing and only persisted because a friend urged him to. Eventually he succeeded as an undergraduate and as a graduate student. He encouraged students to attribute poor performance to not making enough effort. He also encouraged them to attribute good performance to making appropriate effort and to ability. He explained that students can change the amount of effort they devote to a task and that a major component of successful effort is persistence. Finally, he emphasized that long-term effort improves ability.

Another group of internalizers and externalizers had the same lecture, but they did not see the videotape. After the lecture, all students were given homework unrelated to the lecture and were told that they would be tested on the homework and the lecture in a week. The results showed that the videotape improved the performance of externalizers on both the homework and lecture tests. Both internalizers and externalizers who saw the videotape performed better on the homework and lecture tests than students who did not see the videotape.

Classroom Applications

Specifically acknowledge when students make sincere efforts and when they use effective and/or ineffective strategies. It is often difficult for students to be aware of their physical growth or, for that matter, of their learning achievement (or growth). Every once in a while, it would be wise for a teacher to demonstrate this growth to students. Feedback on growth should include progress in understanding, remembering and applying specific concepts, strategies, and skills. There are various ways that this can be done. Give a pretest and posttest. Videotape students working at the beginning, middle, and end of a unit of study. In either case, students can see for themselves their achievement and that they themselves were largely responsible for the progress. Take, for example, the solution of a quadratic inequality. At first sight, it would clearly be confusing, and this confusion, often frustrating, should be gently documented. If possible, this process of dissecting the quadratic into factors, inspecting their relationship to the original quadratic, graphing the result, and through several exercises showing a clear ability to solve quadratic inequalities, gives the teacher ample ammunition to convince students that through their efforts achievement is possible and that they control it.

Precautions and Possible Pitfalls

Teachers should take care to make these external "interferences" (pretest, posttest, video taping, and so forth) as unobtrusive as possible so that they document normal behaviors. Furthermore, the teacher should constantly bear in mind the goal of the assessment, that it is not a rating device, but rather one that serves a very specific goal, namely, demonstrating to students that there has been genuine learning taking place and, for the most part, they are responsible for that growth.

Some students develop feelings of hopelessness or helplessness from repeated poor performance in mathematics. These students tend to doubt that they have the ability to succeed in mathematics. These students, in particular, need special attention in developing the feeling that they have the power to improve their performance by making persistent efforts and by using more effective strategies.

SOURCE

Perry, R. P., & Penner, K. S. (1990). Enhancing academic achievement in college students through attributional retraining and instruction. *Journal of Educational Psychology, 82*(2), 262-271.

THE TIP (1.29)

Help students learn without relying on teacher-centered approaches. Give them carefully chosen sequences of worked-out examples and problems to solve.

What the Research Says

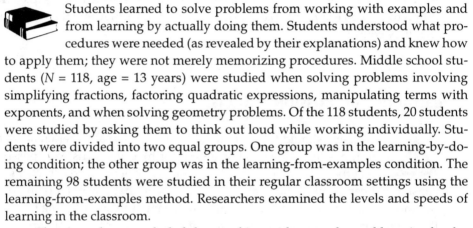

Students learned to solve problems from working with examples and from learning by actually doing them. Students understood what procedures were needed (as revealed by their explanations) and knew how to apply them; they were not merely memorizing procedures. Middle school students (N = 118, age = 13 years) were studied when solving problems involving simplifying fractions, factoring quadratic expressions, manipulating terms with exponents, and when solving geometry problems. Of the 118 students, 20 students were studied by asking them to think out loud while working individually. Students were divided into two equal groups. One group was in the learning-by-doing condition; the other group was in the learning-from-examples condition. The remaining 98 students were studied in their regular classroom settings using the learning-from-examples method. Researchers examined the levels and speeds of learning in the classroom.

The researchers concluded that working with examples and learning by doing are effective alternatives to teacher-centered instructional approaches such as lecturing or other methods of direct instruction.

Classroom Applications

Perhaps a fine illustration of where the lecture method works worst is in the instruction of problem solving. Although problem solving has continuously been stressed for importance by the NCTM since before it issued its *Agenda for Action* in 1980 and then, of course, in its *Standards* in 1989, it is often a neglected topic in the curriculum. Problem solving is a very individual activity. Everyone learns at his or her own pace and with a different experiential background. Therefore, it is not advisable for the teacher to teach this topic through lecture. By providing students with model solutions, after they have had time to try to solve (or actually solve) a problem, you enable the student to focus on the various parts and skills of the solution on their own terms and at their own pace. This allows the student to enjoy the solution and then to ponder over its cleverness, with the hope that this will allow a deeper appreciation for the work and for replication in the near future.

Like the musician trying to play at Carnegie Hall, to be good problem solvers, students need practice, practice, and more practice! Learning to solve problems by doing the problems rather than watching and listening to the teacher is an important ingredient of success.

Precautions and Possible Pitfalls

Needless to say, examples provided must be appropriate and the problems must be in a carefully arranged sequence. Then it is of utmost importance to discuss the solution with the student. Perhaps showing the alternative solutions, or discussing possible pitfalls set by the problem-poser for the student, will allow a deeper appreciation for the solution and make for a more genuine learning experience.

SOURCE

Zhu, X., & Simon, H. A. (1987). Learning mathematics from examples and by doing. *Cognition and Instruction, 4*(3), 137-166.

THE TIP (1.30)

 Help students understand their own thought processes and guide them in learning to think like mathematicians.

What the Research Says

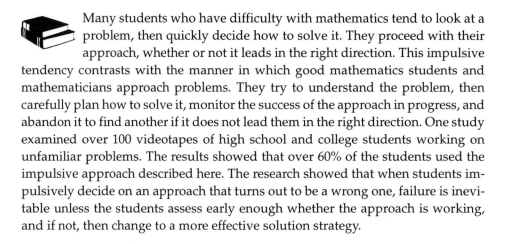 Many students who have difficulty with mathematics tend to look at a problem, then quickly decide how to solve it. They proceed with their approach, whether or not it leads in the right direction. This impulsive tendency contrasts with the manner in which good mathematics students and mathematicians approach problems. They try to understand the problem, then carefully plan how to solve it, monitor the success of the approach in progress, and abandon it to find another if it does not lead them in the right direction. One study examined over 100 videotapes of high school and college students working on unfamiliar problems. The results showed that over 60% of the students used the impulsive approach described here. The research showed that when students impulsively decide on an approach that turns out to be a wrong one, failure is inevitable unless the students assess early enough whether the approach is working, and if not, then change to a more effective solution strategy.

Classroom Applications

 To help students become more aware of and take more control over their own thinking, teachers can coach or guide their thinking process so it becomes more like that of a mathematician. Such guidance or coaching can occur by asking them

1. How this one solution approach would apply to another problem?

2. Exactly what are they doing?

3. Why are they using this particular approach to solve this problem?

4. How do they know whether the approach is leading in the right direction?

5. Is there is any other way of solving this problem?

6. How they will know if the answer they get is right?

7. What will they do with the answer once they get it?

Precautions and Possible Pitfalls

 Teachers should take individual differences into account when applying the ideas listed here. Students come to the classroom with very different learning habits and needs; this list may have to be modified, supplemented, or both to take student differences into account.

SOURCE

Schoenfeld, A. H. (1989). Teaching mathematical thinking and problem solving. In L. B. Resnick & L. Klopfer (Eds.), *Toward the thinking curriculum: Current cognitive research* (pp. 83–103). Alexandria, VA: Yearbook of the Association for Supervision and Curriculum Development.

THE TIP (1.31)

 Adolescents need extended support for acquiring the ability to visualize.

What the Research Says

Boys and girls, during infancy, childhood, adolescence, or all of these, impart and acquire knowledge and emotions mainly in kinesthetic and auditory ways. This is very clear when you think of the way children or young people communicate. They speak in very plain, harsh terms and corroborate their words with slapping someone's back, giving a light shove, or making other gestures involving big motions.

In general there are four methods of visualizing:

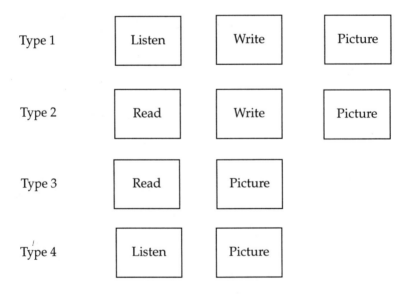

Type 1	Listen	Write	Picture
Type 2	Read	Write	Picture
Type 3	Read	Picture	
Type 4	Listen	Picture	

Previous research has shown that students who use all four types of visualization will learn more easily in school than students who remember only through auditory methods. Students who especially like the fourth type are very often regarded as gifted. Research has shown that above all, urban students are auditory learners. Research also has shown that the ability to visualize does not develop by itself.

Classroom Applications

 In addition to applying sketches and pictures during lessons, the nonverbal performance of the teacher is decisive for student's ability to visualizing. The way a teacher speaks can improve students' visualizing—whether the students are already advanced in visualizing or not.

Precautions and Possible Pitfalls

 These hints are for you to use when you want to help students imagine pictures. In many other situations, the same hint can be a handicap! For instance, if you have trouble with the discipline of some students, it is more useful to use body language than to speak softly and in long sentences. Do not consider the recommendations for nonverbal behavior as applicable in general.

SOURCE

Grinder, M. (1992). *NLP für Lehrer. Ein praxisorientiertes Arbeitsbuch* [*NLP for teachers. A praxis-orientated workbook*]. Freiburg im Breisgau, Germany: Verlag für Angewandte Kinesiologie GmbH.

THE TIP (1.32)

 Encourage students to be mentally active while reading their textbooks.

What the Research Says

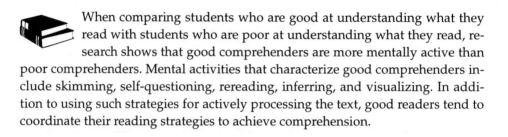 When comparing students who are good at understanding what they read with students who are poor at understanding what they read, research shows that good comprehenders are more mentally active than poor comprehenders. Mental activities that characterize good comprehenders include skimming, self-questioning, rereading, inferring, and visualizing. In addition to using such strategies for actively processing the text, good readers tend to coordinate their reading strategies to achieve comprehension.

Classroom Applications

It is unfortunate that most students do not use their mathematics textbook in the way authors would like them to be used. Typically, students only use textbooks to complete homework assignments or to prepare for a test. This use shortchanges many students, for the textbook could very well (and often does) provide alternative explanations to a concept explained by the teacher in class. Students would be well advised (and should even be urged) to read the explanatory material covered in class, for it is quite conceivable that a student's notes are not always complete or truly reliable. Reading a mathematics book is clearly not like reading a novel. The teacher ought to take time out from the normal mathematics instructional program to focus on the way a mathematics textbook ought to be read. By taking a small snippet of time from each of a series of lessons to consider the textbook and how it should be used, the teacher will be making the review (via the textbook) of future topics studied much more effective. The teacher should explain the notation and style of the author, should indicate the author's pedagogical intentions, and any other peculiarities that may be appropriate. Teachers should also help students develop the analytical skills for identifying when, why, and how a particular model described in the text fits a particular problem. The student must constantly question his or her understanding of each idea and look toward the overriding direction or "big picture" of the concepts or unit being developed and how they are related to other concepts. Often, mathematics textbooks offer model solutions to problems. These should also be read in a very active fashion before doing the exercises, even if the student thinks he or she can "fly" through the exercises after or without reading the explanatory material.

Precautions and Possible Pitfalls

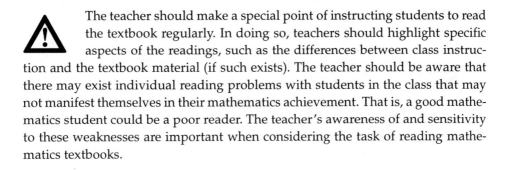 The teacher should make a special point of instructing students to read the textbook regularly. In doing so, teachers should highlight specific aspects of the readings, such as the differences between class instruction and the textbook material (if such exists). The teacher should be aware that there may exist individual reading problems with students in the class that may not manifest themselves in their mathematics achievement. That is, a good mathematics student could be a poor reader. The teacher's awareness of and sensitivity to these weaknesses are important when considering the task of reading mathematics textbooks.

SOURCE

Long, J. D., & Long, E. W. (1987). Enhancing student achievement through meta-comprehension training. *Journal of Developmental Education, 11*(1) 2- 5.

THE TIP (1.33)

 Work directly with individual students as often as possible.

What the Research Says

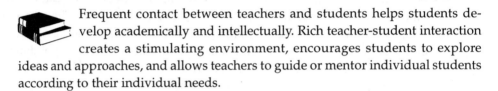 Frequent contact between teachers and students helps students develop academically and intellectually. Rich teacher-student interaction creates a stimulating environment, encourages students to explore ideas and approaches, and allows teachers to guide or mentor individual students according to their individual needs.

Classroom Applications

Working with individual students in a traditional classroom setting is not practical for long periods of time. While students are working individually on an exercise, the teacher should visit with individual students and offer them some meaningful suggestions. Such suggestions might include hints on moving a student, who appears frustrated or bogged down on a point, toward a solution. These private comments to students might also be in the form of advice regarding the form of the student's work. That is, some students are "their own worst enemy" when they are doing a geometry problem and working with a diagram that is either so small that they cannot do anything worthwhile with it, or is so inaccurately drawn that it, too, proves to be relatively useless. Such small support offerings will move students along and give them that very important feeling of teacher interest.

In some cases, when a student experiences more severe problems, the teacher might be wise to work with individual students after classroom hours. In the latter situation, it would be advisable to have the student describe his work as it is being done, trying to justify his procedure and explain concepts. During such one-on-one tutoring sessions, the teacher can get a good insight into the student's problems. Are they conceptual? Has the student missed understanding an algorithm? Does he have perceptual difficulties? Spatial difficulties? And so on.

Precautions and Possible Pitfalls

To work with individual students and merely make perfunctory comments when more might be expected could be useless when considering that the severity of a possible problem might warrant more attention. Teachers should make every effort to give proper attention to students when reacting to this teaching tip. They should keep the student's level in mind so that where appropriate, teachers can add some spice to the individual sessions by providing carefully selected challenges to the student so that there may be a further individualization in the learning process. Make sure good students don't get bored. Challenge them by giving them more difficult problems to solve, having them tutor other students, or having them evaluate alternative approaches to solving a problem.

SOURCE

Pressley, M., & McCormick, C. (1995). *Advanced educational psychology*. New York: HarperCollins.

THE TIP (1.34)

 Have students study written model solutions to problems while learning and practicing problem solving.

What the Research Says

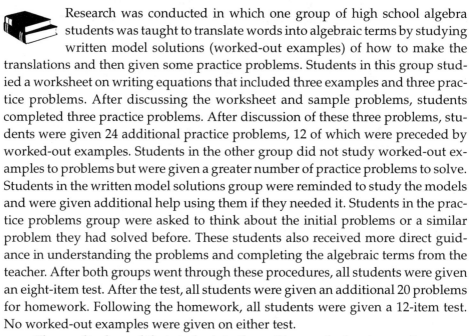 Research was conducted in which one group of high school algebra students was taught to translate words into algebraic terms by studying written model solutions (worked-out examples) of how to make the translations and then given some practice problems. Students in this group studied a worksheet on writing equations that included three examples and three practice problems. After discussing the worksheet and sample problems, students completed three practice problems. After discussion of these three problems, students were given 24 additional practice problems, 12 of which were preceded by worked-out examples. Students in the other group did not study worked-out examples to problems but were given a greater number of practice problems to solve. Students in the written model solutions group were reminded to study the models and were given additional help using them if they needed it. Students in the practice problems group were asked to think about the initial problems or a similar problem they had solved before. These students also received more direct guidance in understanding the problems and completing the algebraic terms from the teacher. After both groups went through these procedures, all students were given an eight-item test. After the test, all students were given an additional 20 problems for homework. Following the homework, all students were given a 12-item test. No worked-out examples were given on either test.

The results showed that students in the written worked-out examples group made fewer errors on both tests; they completed their problems faster and with less help than students in the practice-only group.

Classroom Applications

Written model solutions to problems can be used as supports for homework, when doing individual instruction with remedial students, and in regular classroom instruction. Teachers should help students understand why and how a particular model fits a particular problem. Students ought to use worked-out examples with comprehension, rather than employ rote memorization. Exercises that provide practice with algebraic skills lend themselves quite well to this scheme. Because the skills tend to be repetitive and similar, referring back to the model solution will be an important form of review and reinforcement of procedures. Although this sort of recollection is not considered real problem solving, it does provide some students with the necessary support to learn mathematical skills. It should be noted that real problem solving is also dependent to some extent on recalling previous problem-solving experiences. These sometimes manifest themselves as cleverly solved "model solutions." Thus, models, albeit at a higher level, similarly serve to provide a positive experience for mathematics students. There is a school of thought that believes that much of what one does in school mathematics is recalling prior examples of the same or similar situations.

Precautions and Possible Pitfalls

To use model solutions for a particular type of verbal problem can also be counterproductive in that it could set students up for solving any problem that looks like the model in the same way as the model. In real life, problems can subtly differ, and if a student is too dependent on seeing a model solution beforehand, it could diminish his or her creativeness in problem solving.

SOURCE

Carroll, W. (1994). Using worked-out examples as an instructional support in the algebra classroom. *Journal of Educational Psychology, 86*(3), 360-367.

THE TIP (1.35)

 Does grade skipping hurt mathematically talented students socially and emotionally? Don't worry about accelerating your talented students!

What the Research Says

Researchers conducted a long-term study of hundreds of male and female students who were identified as mathematically precocious youths in a talent search. The study began when students were 12-14 years of age and continued until they were age 23. The researchers examined the effects of the type and amount of acceleration students received on their social and emotional development. Two types of acceleration were examined: the number of grades skipped in school (grade acceleration) and the number of advanced placement, college courses, or both enrolled in while in high school (subject matter acceleration). A questionnaire was administered to assess four areas of social and emotional development: self-esteem, self-acceptance/identity, social interaction, and locus of control (whether they internalize or externalize responsibility for their outcomes). Students were assessed when they were 18 and again when they were 23. The results indicated that acceleration did not affect students socially or emotionally. In addition, there were no differences between males and females.

Classroom Applications

Subject matter acceleration, when done creatively, can bear some interesting fruit. There is not much creativity in accelerating a student along an already established ladder of courses in mathematics. Yet, under such a scheme, special care must be taken to avoid some common pitfalls (see text that follows). Again, to simply provide the student with the regular course work at a faster pace does little beyond keeping the student continuously challenged. Another form of acceleration might be to move the student along more quickly, while at the same time, offering him or her the opportunity to investigate the curriculum topics in a broader sense. For example, when studying the Pythagorean Theorem, rather than investigating the theorem and its traditional applications and then moving on to the next topic in the syllabus, it might be worthwhile to have the student investigate the Pythagorean Theorem's extensions beyond the right triangle to acute triangles ($a^2 + b^2 > c^2$) and to obtuse triangles ($a^2 + b^2 < c^2$).

The student can also consider the extension to the Pythagorean to three dimensions, or to other fields such as number theory, where the nature of Pythagorean numbers is studied.

Precautions and Possible Pitfalls

One of the most serious problems attached to grade and subject matter acceleration is that of sending a student through a set curriculum so fast that he doesn't truly get the full flavor of the subject matter, but rather just moves along to finish it as quickly as possible. Another point to consider is the problem of accelerating a student along so quickly that he or she finishes all that the school has to offer in mathematics and is then left without any further mathematics to study and yet still in high school finishing other courses. Such a "vacation" from mathematics will have a very deleterious effect on the future of a talented student, who could then be "lost" to the field of mathematics. One way to avoid this is either to provide him or her with an independent study program under the tutelage of a teacher or to enroll in an appropriate mathematics course at a nearby college. These considerations should be addressed before an acceleration program commences.

SOURCE

Richardson, T. M., & Persson Benbow, C. (1990). Long-term effects of acceleration on the social-emotional adjustment of mathematically precocious youths. *Journal of Educational Psychology, 82*(3), 464-470.

THE TIP (1.36)

 Emphasize higher-level thinking objectives in regular mathematics classes so that all students incorporate the features of enriched academic and honors classes.

What the Research Says

A study was conducted in 16 high schools with 1,205 classes of 303 teachers in California and Michigan. Grade levels ranged from 9-12. Teachers were asked to specify their instructional goals for each of their classes. The results showed that enriched classes emphasize high-level thinking objectives such as understanding the logical structure of mathematics, understanding the nature of proof, knowing mathematical principles and algorithms, and thinking about what a problem means and the ways it might be solved. In contrast, regular mathematics classes tended to emphasize lower-level thinking objectives such as memorizing facts, rules, and steps; performing computations with speed and accuracy; and developing an awareness of the importance of mathematics in everyday life.

Classroom Applications

Enrichment is not reserved for the gifted! There are many topics that are "off the beaten path" and that can be made suitable for an average ability class, and even a low ability class. The trick is to have the sensitivity to make these content adjustments. For example, students in lower-level classes, who are still struggling with numerical facts, or arithmetic algorithms, or perhaps with some simple algebraic skills, could benefit greatly by having teachers digress to consider the nature of parity of numbers, or to consider an arithmetic short-cut, which has some nifty mathematical justifications. These digressions exhibit a modicum of higher-order thinking skills. Such activities serve to enrich the instructional program both in the thinking skills provoked as well as the topics considered. Such digressions, or enrichment ideas, can be found in many sources. Some of these are under the rubric of "recreational mathematics," which can be found in books designed for mathematics teachers. One such book is *Teaching Secondary School Mathematics: Techniques and Enrichment Units* by A. S. Posamentier and J. Stepelman (1998).

Precautions and Possible Pitfalls

Perhaps the most important precaution when enriching a mathematics class (besides selecting appropriate material) is to be sure not to underestimate your students! Also, don't overemphasize the importance of the enrichment activity or it might render the regular instructional program less interesting. This would defeat the purpose of this enrichment activity: to motivate students toward further study in mathematics.

SOURCE

Raudenbush, S., Rowan, G., & Cheong, Y. F. (1993). Higher-order instructional goals in secondary schools: Class, teacher, and school influences. *American Educational Research Journal, 30*(3), 523-553.

THE TIP (1.37)

 Make sure students pay attention to the feedback you give them.

What the Research Says

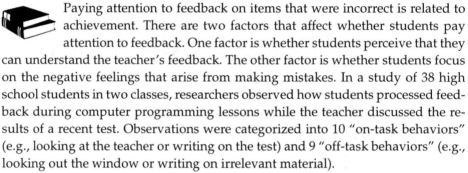 Paying attention to feedback on items that were incorrect is related to achievement. There are two factors that affect whether students pay attention to feedback. One factor is whether students perceive that they can understand the teacher's feedback. The other factor is whether students focus on the negative feelings that arise from making mistakes. In a study of 38 high school students in two classes, researchers observed how students processed feedback during computer programming lessons while the teacher discussed the results of a recent test. Observations were categorized into 10 "on-task behaviors" (e.g., looking at the teacher or writing on the test) and 9 "off-task behaviors" (e.g., looking out the window or writing on irrelevant material).

Thirteen low- and high-achieving students were randomly selected for interviews to get more detailed information on how they processed feedback. One distinct pattern that frequently emerged was students' judgment that they could not understand the teacher's feedback. When students do understand the feedback, they listen to what the teacher is saying and try to figure out what they did wrong. When they do not understand the teacher's feedback, they tune out. The other pattern that emerged, but was less common, was getting upset about making errors. When this occurred, instead of focusing on the problem, students tended to focus on their negative feelings.

Classroom Applications

Perhaps the best way to assure that a teacher's feedback is heeded is to have the students write about their error: what it was, why they made it, and how they would now solve the problem involved in the situation addressed by the teacher. For example, when a student could not do a proof of a particular geometric theorem, the teacher should expect the student to write about the correction and then demonstrate with another theorem that this problematic situation is now relieved. A student who just got some useful feedback from the teacher may also be asked to do a future and similar problem on the chalkboard and discuss it with the rest of the class. This will ensure that a student understands what the teacher has told him or her and not just gloss over the response just to get the teacher "off his or her back." Another strategy is for teachers to have students keep a journal of their errors and regularly make journal entries when getting corrected papers returned or when reviewing work orally in class.

Precautions and Possible Pitfalls

Teachers should be aware of the fact that some of their comments, whether given individually or to the class, may be ignored or simply forgotten. Simple awareness of the importance of the students retaining teacher feedback is already one big step in making this aspect of the instructional program effective. Journal entries, written error analyses, or both can become tedious and should take on various forms. For example, the student might see this additional written assignment as a form of punishment. If this is sensed by the teacher, there should be an alternative way of reaching the same objective. In this case, the teacher may have the student who got the teacher feedback explain the problem and the teacher resolution to a classmate.

SOURCE

Gagne, E. D., Crutcher, R. J., Anzelc, J., Geisman, C., Hoffman, V., Schutz, P., & Lizcano, L. (1987). The role of student processing of feedback in classroom achievement. *Cognition and Instruction, 4*(3), 167-186.

THE TIP (1.38)

 Give students the kind of feedback that will most help them improve their future performance.

What the Research Says

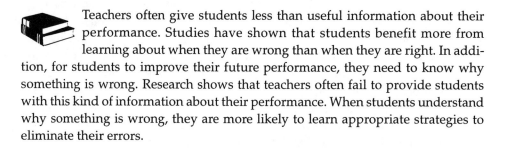 Teachers often give students less than useful information about their performance. Studies have shown that students benefit more from learning about when they are wrong than when they are right. In addition, for students to improve their future performance, they need to know why something is wrong. Research shows that teachers often fail to provide students with this kind of information about their performance. When students understand why something is wrong, they are more likely to learn appropriate strategies to eliminate their errors.

Classroom Applications

Mathematics instruction, in general, has lots of opportunities to give a right answer or a wrong answer. The "gray area" hardly exists. For a teacher to merely indicate the right answer, or to indicate that a student's response is wrong, does little to aim the student in the right direction. Teachers should analyze incorrect responses to see if the errors are in reasoning, incorrect interpretations, faulty work with algorithms, or the like. Often, such an analysis can be time consuming, but extremely worthwhile, for it is the discovery of the error (resulting from their error analysis) that can be the key to helping a student sort out his mathematics difficulties.

There are several types of errors that occur in the normal mathematics classroom. First, there are the errors that are common to a large portion of the class. These can be attributable to a misunderstanding in class or to some prior learning (common to most of the class) that causes students to similarly react incorrectly to a specific situation. When the teacher notices this sort of thing, a general remark and clarification to the entire class would be appropriate. The misconception may be one of not understanding a concept, such as the average of rates not being treated as the arithmetic mean (because it is, in fact, the harmonic mean). Or it could involve the incorrect use of the quadratic formula by a number of students who carelessly do not draw their fraction bar long enough to include the numerator – *b*. Often, errors are simply due to careless mistakes. Teachers should help students develop and implement specific correction plans to prevent their errors from recurring in the future. We direct the reader to a pertinent discussion of student errors, "The Logic of Error," by Dr. Ethan Akin in *The Art of Problem Solving: A Resource for the Mathematics Teacher*, edited by A. S. Posamentier and W. Schulz (1996).

Precautions and Possible Pitfalls

 It is possible that through an error analysis of a student's work, several errors may turn up. To point out too many faults at one time could confound the student and consequently have a counterproductive effect. The teacher should arrange the discovered errors in order of importance, and successively discuss them with the student one by one, going on to the next one only after successful completion of the earlier one. Teachers should follow up to see if students have successfully followed their error correction plans and have rectified previous errors, especially recurring errors.

SOURCE

Bangert-Drowns, R. L., Kulik, C. C., Kulik, J. A., & Morgan, M. (1991). The instructional effect of feedback in test-like events. *Review of Educational Research, 61*, 213-238.

THE TIP (1.39)

 Promptly give students information or feedback about their performance.

What the Research Says

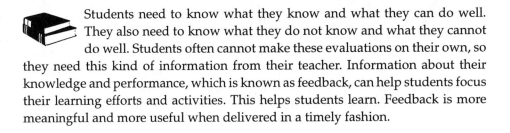 Students need to know what they know and what they can do well. They also need to know what they do not know and what they cannot do well. Students often cannot make these evaluations on their own, so they need this kind of information from their teacher. Information about their knowledge and performance, which is known as feedback, can help students focus their learning efforts and activities. This helps students learn. Feedback is more meaningful and more useful when delivered in a timely fashion.

Classroom Applications

Homework in the mathematics classroom usually consists of problems with a very definite answer. It is very tempting for teachers to spot-check homework by inspecting to see if the right answers are offered without looking at the method to reach the answer. Whenever possible, teachers should thoroughly examine students' homework answers and methods; they should give students information about the quality of their performance.

If a teacher's class is too large to do a thorough check of the homework, the teacher can select different subgroups from within the class daily, picking their homework from the collected class set. Teachers should carefully inspect the work, focusing more on the method than on merely seeing if the right answer had been obtained, and should provide timely, specific feedback.

Precautions and Possible Pitfalls

 The teacher may either randomly select subgroups or select them by design. In any case, this selection should not be predictable by the students. Otherwise, those who anticipate homework inspection will do a better job and those who don't, won't. If feedback is not provided in a timely fashion, it will be of limited usefulness to students.

SOURCE

Chickering, A., & Gamson, Z. (1987). Seven principles for good practice in undergraduate education. *Wingspread Journal, 9*(2), special insert.

THE TIP (1.40)

 Feedback on practice is essential for improving student performance.

What the Research Says

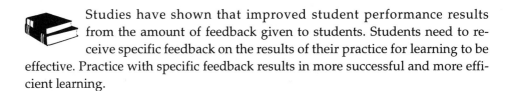 Studies have shown that improved student performance results from the amount of feedback given to students. Students need to receive specific feedback on the results of their practice for learning to be effective. Practice with specific feedback results in more successful and more efficient learning.

Classroom Applications

In a mathematics instruction program, there are many opportunities for practice of the skills presented. By pairing students and having them read each others work, or by having students compare their work to model solutions, a form of feedback can be obtained regularly without a great expense of time. Teachers might also systematically review a small and different sampling of student papers each day, and from this small number of collected papers provide some meaningful feedback to the students. For example, suppose that a classroom is situated in rows of students. The teacher may "at random" call for the papers of everyone sitting in the first seat of each row, or from the students sitting on the diagonal, or from everyone in the third row. If a teacher wants to check on a particular student's paper a second day, because there may be some serious questions about the student's work, then the teacher can ask for the student's paper by including him or her in the second day's set of collected papers. This can be done by calling on that set that also describes his or her seat. For example, select the third row of students one day and then the next day, because the target student is sitting in the last seat of the row, select the papers from all students sitting in the last seat of each row. This would "inadvertently" include the target student a second time.

Because it is unreasonable to expect the teacher to do a thorough reading of everyone's paper every day, there are alternative ways to get feedback to students on their homework. One could search for parent volunteers, retired teachers, or both, who might like to take on some part-time work reading and reacting (in writing) to student work. One might also try to engage some older and more advanced students to undertake a similar activity, using a "cross-age" tutoring approach. This would also serve the more advanced students well because they can benefit by looking back over previously learned material from a more advanced standpoint. By doing this, not only are the target students being helped but the older student is deepening his or her knowledge of mathematics.

Precautions and Possible Pitfalls

 Teachers often do not have sufficient resources to provide individual feedback to each student. When having students give each other feedback, teachers should be aware that the feedback from students will be of a different nature and certainly not a replacement for that provided by the teacher. Student feedback must be monitored to avoid perpetuating flawed ideas or misconceptions. The same holds true for teachers' aides, parent volunteers, or retirees assisting in the classroom.

SOURCE

Benjamin, L. T., & Lowman, K. D. (Eds.). (1981). *Activities handbook for the teaching of psychology.* Washington, DC: American Psychological Association.

THE TIP (1.41)

Don't give students graded feedback on their performance too early.

What the Research Says

 Giving grades early stimulates students to participate actively in their lessons, but may undermine achievement in the long run. Previous research provided evidence that students learn because of anxiety over grades or because they get good grades with a minimum of effort. Giving grades early is especially beneficial for students who require more time to understand things. They tend to be afraid of saying something wrong and of getting bad grades. Early grading is not viewed as being judgmental about a student's knowledge. It is viewed more as informative rather than as judgmental.

This study investigated four 9th-grade classes on the effects of giving grades at an early stage of knowledge acquisition. To show the effects of early grading, four classes were separated into two groups. Both groups received computer-aided instruction and received a grade after every step. The first group did not get to know about their grades; the second group was informed about their grades. The achievements of the groups were compared on the basis of the grade after every step and on a final test. Students who knew their grades did slightly better on the interim tests. Their learning was enhanced by the grades. In contrast, on the final test, students who did not know their interim grades did noticeably better. They were not pushed by the pressure of grades. They used additional work to develop self-control. In this way, they dealt with the issue of their learning needs, they understood it profoundly, and achieved at higher levels.

Classroom Applications

Avoid giving grades at an early stage of learning. Students who are not interested in a particular topic or even the whole subject can easily get frustrated by early grades, and their motivation can sink even further. On the other hand, early low or mediocre grades can promote rapid success. In some cases, however, this leads to students resting on their laurels. During the period when students are acquiring new knowledge, use grades sparingly.

Precautions and Possible Pitfalls

Do not stop all assessment during the early stage. First, you, as teacher, need to evaluate their performance, then students need assessment to evaluate or at least estimate their own achievement. In addition, you will always find some students who are entirely motivated by grades. Therefore, during the early learning phase, you should use oral or nonverbal assessment techniques.

SOURCE

Lechner, H. J., Brehm, R.-I., & Zbigniew, M. (1996). Zensierung und ihr Einfluß auf die Leistung der Schüler [Influence of marks on student's achievements]. *Pädagogik und Schulalltag, 51*(3), 371-379

THE TIP (1.42)

 Use analogies to help students develop more valid conceptions.

What the Research Says

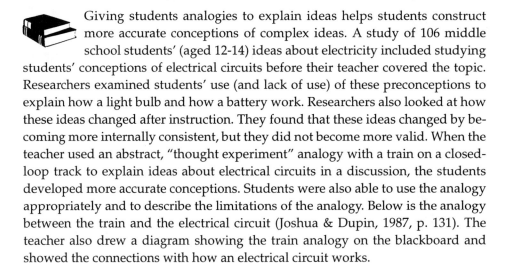 Giving students analogies to explain ideas helps students construct more accurate conceptions of complex ideas. A study of 106 middle school students' (aged 12-14) ideas about electricity included studying students' conceptions of electrical circuits before their teacher covered the topic. Researchers examined students' use (and lack of use) of these preconceptions to explain how a light bulb and how a battery work. Researchers also looked at how these ideas changed after instruction. They found that these ideas changed by becoming more internally consistent, but they did not become more valid. When the teacher used an abstract, "thought experiment" analogy with a train on a closed-loop track to explain ideas about electrical circuits in a discussion, the students developed more accurate conceptions. Students were also able to use the analogy appropriately and to describe the limitations of the analogy. Below is the analogy between the train and the electrical circuit (Joshua & Dupin, 1987, p. 131). The teacher also drew a diagram showing the train analogy on the blackboard and showed the connections with how an electrical circuit works.

TRAIN	ELECTRICAL CIRCUIT
Cars	Electrons
Movement of cars	Movement of electrons
Rate at which cars pass a certain point along the track	Rate at which electrons pass a given point in the circuit (current intensity)
Mechanical friction (obstacle in the track)	Electrical resistance (atomic nuclei)
Men pushing train	Battery
Muscular fatigue of men	Wearing out of the battery
Vibrations of the cars, noise and heat produced by collisions with obstacle on the track	Heat in the wires and battery, heat and light in the bulb produced by the interactions of the electrons and atomic nuclei

Classroom Applications

1. Do a concrete, hands-on classroom activity that involves the concept you are trying to teach, and follow it with a discussion.

2. Through the discussion, identify students' preinstructional ideas about the concept.

3. Make sure students are aware of the different interpretations of the same concepts.

4. Have students evaluate the competing interpretations.

5. Give students a task that enables them to test out and decide between these interpretations and will also help them to develop new interpretations, to refine old interpretations, or both, as needed.

6. Have students draw conclusions based on this task. Help them identify and try to reconcile major contradictions.

7. Give students an analogy to the concept. Have them discuss the analogy, including its relevance and limitations.

In mathematics, finding analogies to use for developing more accurate conceptions may be more difficult because the material is more abstract and skill oriented. One possible example, however, of where a model may simulate an abstract concept is to discuss the concept of a function using the model of a gun shooting bullets at a target. The bullets comprise the "domain" and the target comprises the "range." The gun, and its aiming, is the function. Because a bullet can be used only once, we know that the elements in the domain can be used only once. The gun can hit the same point on the target more than once; therefore, points in the range can be used more than once. Some points on the target may never be hit; yet, all the bullets are used. Thus, a function is a mapping of all points of the domain to points in the range. When all the points on the target are hit, then the function is an "onto" function; when each point in the range is used only once, then we have a "1 – 1" function. We have a "1 – 1 onto" function when both properties are attained. This is also called a "1 – 1 correspondence." Using the-gun-shooting-the-target analogy makes the concepts of function, domain, and range easier for students to understand and remember.

Precautions and Possible Pitfalls

Students often have difficulty fitting new ideas into preexisting frameworks. Make sure the preexisting framework is very clear before proceeding to use it as an analogy. Students must have a clear understanding of the framework to be used in the analogy, such as a gun shooting bullets at the target, for the analogy to be a useful tool for understanding the mathematical concepts, such as function, domain, and range.

SOURCE

Joshua, S., & Dupin, J. J. (1987). Taking into account student conceptions in instructional strategy: An example in physics. *Cognition and Instruction, 4*(2), 117-135.

THE TIP (1.43)

 Use a three-step inductive technique to identify and over-come students' misconceptions about mathematics.

What the Research Says

Students do not come as "blank slates" to their mathematics classes. They tend to have many complex ideas about mathematics, some of which are valid and some of which are not valid. Numerous studies have shown that students have many "naive theories," preconceptions, or misconceptions about mathematics that interfere with their learning. There are so many mathematical misconceptions that they have been compiled into a resource book. A three-step inductive technique has been found to be effective in helping teachers identify and overcome students' mathematical misconceptions.

Classroom Applications

Sample problem: Write an equation using the variables S and T to represent the following statement: "There are six times as many students as teachers in this school." The following three-step inductive technique has been found to help teachers identify and overcome students' mathematical misconceptions:

1. Probe for qualitative understanding. Look for linguistic confusion and naive misconceptions. For example, ask, "Are there more teachers or students in this school?"

2. Probe for quantitative understanding. If students understand there are more students than teachers, look for understanding of the quantitative implications. For example, ask, "If there were 10 teachers in the school, how many students would there be?"

3. Probe for conceptual understanding.

   a. Have students write an equation. Look for common patterns of errors. For example, many students write: $6S = T$;

   b. Induce conflict. For example, ask, "If you substitute $S = 60$ in your equation, would you get $T = 10$ as before?"

Precautions and Possible Pitfalls

 Because students have actively constructed their misconceptions from their everyday experiences, they are very attached to them and find them very difficult to give up. Therefore, it is important to create situations in which students are confronted with their misconceptions and are allowed (with guidance) to discover them and replace them with valid conceptions.

SOURCE

Lochead, J., & Mestre, J. (1988). From words to algebra: Mending misconceptions. In A. Coxford & A. Schulte (Eds.), *The ideas of algebra, K-12* (pp. 127-135). Reston, VA: National Council of Mathematics Teachers.

RESOURCE BOOK OF MATHEMATICAL MISCONCEPTIONS

Benander, L., & Clement, J. (1985). *Catalogue of error patterns observed in courses on basic mathematics* (Internal Report No. 115). Amherst: University of Massachusetts, Scientific Reasoning Research Institute, Hasboruck Laboratory. (ERIC Document Reproduction Service No. ED 287 762)

THE TIP (1.44)

 Structure teaching of mathematical concepts and skills around problems to be solved, using a problem-centered or problem-based approach to learning.

What the Research Says

Problem-centered or problem-based learning is becoming recognized as an outstanding way of teaching both content and problem-solving skills. One study compared six classes that received problem-centered mathematics instruction for 2 years with students who received problem-centered mathematics instruction for one year and with students who received traditional textbook-based instruction. Researchers examined students' performance on standardized achievement tests and investigated students' personal goals and beliefs about the reasons for their success in mathematics. The results showed that students who received problem-centered instruction for 2 years demonstrated significantly higher mathematics achievement than traditionally instructed students—both in their proficiency in solving problems and their conceptual understanding. In addition, problem-centered learning students had stronger beliefs than traditional students about the importance of finding not only *different* ways of solving problems, but the importance of finding *their own ways* of solving problems. Students, who received problem-centered mathematics instruction for only one year and then returned to textbook teaching, performed at levels comparable to the textbook-only instruction students. Consequently, to achieve meaningful benefits from the problem-centered approach, students should receive more than one year of instruction using this form of teaching. This problem-centered type of approach has become a standard instructional practice in many medical school programs.

Classroom Applications

Instead of starting a unit by using the textbook and telling students about a mathematical topic; explaining and demonstrating various concepts, problems, and solution methods; start by giving students a meaningful problem to solve. Problem-centered or problem-based learning is a method of teaching that uses ill-structured, real-world problems as the context for learning basic content through in-depth investigations. To solve the problem, students will need to learn specific mathematical concepts and solution strategies.

Teachers only provide students with enough information to enable them to begin their inquiry. They never give students enough information to actually solve a problem. With this instructional method, students cannot simply solve problems by applying a particular formula. There must be student reasoning and inquiry. Often there is more than one way to solve a problem. Students will learn important concepts and skills through mathematical inquiry in a meaningful context. The teacher's role is to be a coach, mentor, or tutor who guides students in their inquiry and helps them develop and understand their own thinking.

One topic, which lends itself to this sort of problem-solving investigation, is the consideration of maxima and minima. For example, students could seek to maximize an area with a given perimeter. They could consider the shape as a variable. They may have it as a rectangle, or a polygon. They may even consider a circle with this given perimeter to see how it compares with the other shapes. This topic can be considered before the study of calculus by inspecting the turning point of a parabola, or by merely inspecting extremes to see the behavior of the variable.

Precautions and Possible Pitfalls

Problems must be at an appropriate level of complexity. In addition, students must have appropriate prior knowledge so they know or can figure out what they need to learn to solve the problem. The topic selected must be appropriate for the ability level of the students, and, above all, it must garner the proper interest among the students. Without this interest, it will not achieve the desired goals.

SOURCE

Checkley, K. (1997). Problem-based learning: The search for solutions to life's messy problems. *Curriculum Update, Summer,* 1-3, 6-8.

Wood, T., & Sellers, P. (1996). Assessment of a problem-centered mathematics program: Don't always call on volunteer responses to teacher questions. Third grade. *Journal of Research in Mathematics Education, 27*(3), 337-353.

Wood, T., & Sellers, P. (1997). Deepening the analysis: Longitudinal assessment, a problem-centered mathematics program. *Journal of Research in Mathematics Education, 28*(2), 163–186.

THE TIP (1.45)

 Although mathematics emphasizes formulas, numbers, geometric objects, and so forth, it is important for you to help your students learn to read and understand their mathematics texts.

What the Research Says

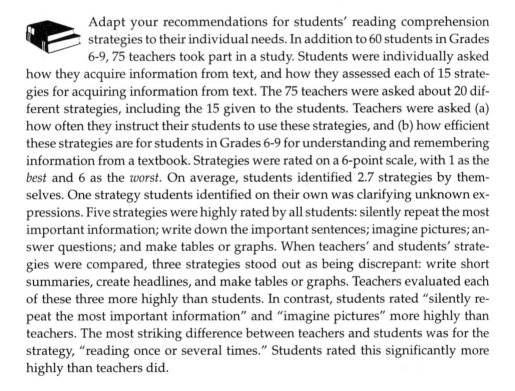

Adapt your recommendations for students' reading comprehension strategies to their individual needs. In addition to 60 students in Grades 6-9, 75 teachers took part in a study. Students were individually asked how they acquire information from text, and how they assessed each of 15 strategies for acquiring information from text. The 75 teachers were asked about 20 different strategies, including the 15 given to the students. Teachers were asked (a) how often they instruct their students to use these strategies, and (b) how efficient these strategies are for students in Grades 6-9 for understanding and remembering information from a textbook. Strategies were rated on a 6-point scale, with 1 as the *best* and 6 as the *worst*. On average, students identified 2.7 strategies by themselves. One strategy students identified on their own was clarifying unknown expressions. Five strategies were highly rated by all students: silently repeat the most important information; write down the important sentences; imagine pictures; answer questions; and make tables or graphs. When teachers' and students' strategies were compared, three strategies stood out as being discrepant: write short summaries, create headlines, and make tables or graphs. Teachers evaluated each of these three more highly than students. In contrast, students rated "silently repeat the most important information" and "imagine pictures" more highly than teachers. The most striking difference between teachers and students was for the strategy, "reading once or several times." Students rated this significantly more highly than teachers did.

Classroom Applications

Students frequently have to deal with reading, even in their mathematics classes. This occurs when new subjects are introduced, summarized, and when assignments are given. To guarantee that all students gain the most from what they read, directly instruct them about the strategies they should implement. For students with learning weaknesses, the following strategies are appropriate:

1. Imagine pictures

2. Write down important sentences

3. Silently repeat the most important information

4. Make tables or graphs

5. Answer questions

6. Underline important words (keywords)

High-achieving students should implement the following strategies:

1. Write short summaries

2. Create headlines

3. Make tables or graphs

4. Draw a comparison with known facts

5. Write down conclusions

Precautions and Possible Pitfalls

Learning reading strategies only in language arts classes does not facilitate success with mathematics. Students tend to compartmentalize what they learn, and cannot be counted on to apply what they learn in their language classes to their reading of mathematics texts or materials.

To apply reading strategies effectively and automatically, students need continuous training and extensive and varied practice (i.e., across subject areas).

SOURCE

Dumke, D., & Wolff-Kollmar, S. (1997). Lernstrategien in der Beurteilung von Lehrern und Schülern [Teachers' and students' evaluation of learning strategies]. *Psychologie in Erziehung und Unterricht, 44*(2), 165-175.

CHAPTER TWO

Social Aspects of the Classroom

THE TIP (2.1)

 Encourage students to work cooperatively with other students.

What the Research Says

When students cooperate with other students, they often get more out of learning than they do when working on their own or even when working with the teacher. When students are isolated from each other and compete with each other, they are less involved in learning, their learning is not as deep, and they have fewer opportunities to improve their thinking. Students who work cooperatively achieve at higher levels, persist longer when working on difficult tasks, and are more motivated to learn because learning becomes fun and meaningful. Cooperative learning also improves self-esteem and social relationships among culturally diverse student populations.

Classroom Applications

Working cooperatively in a mathematics classroom can be done in many ways. Students can be given a challenging problem, and then asked to solve it while working in small groups. Working cooperatively in a group setting, students must verbalize their thoughts and discoveries, which helps them to understand these ideas and use them as steps on the path to a solution. Teachers may present classical challenges such as filling in the cells of a 3×3 grid with the numbers from 1-9 to form a magic square. Or, they may simply ask open-ended questions in which mathematical solutions include judgmental aspects. For example, some "real-life" problems of this nature could be to determine the best location for a railway station location, the minimum sum distance from town to station to town, and other conditions that can be included to describe a "real" situation. These factors present a problem that can be solved in a variety of ways by making judgments about the relative importance of variables. Such open-ended problem situations provide excellent opportunities for students to work cooperatively, probing and prodding each other in their quest for a solution.

Precautions and Possible Pitfalls

Not all group work is cooperative learning! Students must work together, help each other, and learn from each other for it to really be cooperative learning. Beware that one person doesn't dominate the group, which often occurs. Assigning group roles is one way of either preventing this from occurring or correcting it when it does occur. Teachers need to constantly monitor groups as they are solving problems to make sure they stay on task and are working in productive ways.

SOURCE

Johnson, D., & Johnson, R. (1975). *Learning together and alone: Cooperation, competition, and individualization.* Englewood Cliffs, NJ: Prentice Hall.
Davidson, N. (Ed.). (1990). *Cooperative learning in mathematics: A handbook for teachers.* Menlo Park, CA: Addison-Wesley.

THE TIP (2.2)

 Carefully select problems for use in cooperative learning groups.

What the Research Says

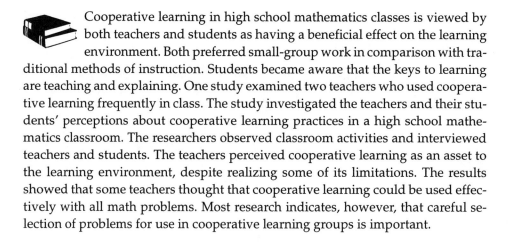 Cooperative learning in high school mathematics classes is viewed by both teachers and students as having a beneficial effect on the learning environment. Both preferred small-group work in comparison with traditional methods of instruction. Students became aware that the keys to learning are teaching and explaining. One study examined two teachers who used cooperative learning frequently in class. The study investigated the teachers and their students' perceptions about cooperative learning practices in a high school mathematics classroom. The researchers observed classroom activities and interviewed teachers and students. The teachers perceived cooperative learning as an asset to the learning environment, despite realizing some of its limitations. The results showed that some teachers thought that cooperative learning could be used effectively with all math problems. Most research indicates, however, that careful selection of problems for use in cooperative learning groups is important.

Classroom Applications

Select problems that are complex enough to require several variables or steps to solve. One example of such an activity in which cooperative learning may be beneficial includes having students investigate (or solve) the following problem:

> A straight railroad track passes nearby two towns. One town is 5 miles from the track while the other is 8 miles from the track. The two towns, which are on the same side of the track, are 18 miles apart from each other. The citizens of the two towns want to build a railroad station somewhere along the track so that it is equally accessible from the two towns. Where should the station be placed?

Discuss the kinds of considerations that might be important in the decision. Explain and justify the geometric solution to the problem. Explain which other variables (not given) might be necessary to give the best location for the station.

Precautions and Possible Pitfalls

Perceptions do not always match reality. When planning to use cooperative learning, be selective about the types of problems or tasks given to the cooperative learning groups. Research on the effectiveness of cooperative learning in mathematics indicates it works more suitably with some math problems and skills rather than others. Teachers' perceptions may not reflect this selectivity, however, and teachers may (unadvisedly) use cooperative learning across the board. Easy problems are unlikely to work effectively in cooperative learning groups because there is less need for students to collaborate and help each other.

SOURCE

Peele, A., & McCoy, L. (1994, April). *Perception of group work in mathematics.* Paper presented at the annual meeting of the American Educational Research Association, New Orleans, LA.

THE TIP (2.3)

Use the "jigsaw" technique (explained in the Classroom Applications section) of cooperative learning as an interesting and effective way for students to learn.

What the Research Says

Contrary to the belief held by some that cooperative learning has only social benefits, research shows that the jigsaw method helps students learn and apply academic content as well. An experimental study was conducted with seven classes of students in Grades 7 and 8. The 141 students were separated into four experimental classes and three control classes. The experimental classes were taught using the jigsaw technique; the three control classes received regular instruction through lectures. The experiment lasted about 4 weeks, with one double lesson per week. This study examined the social, personal, and academic benefits of jigsaw and traditional instruction. Social and personal benefits observed to result from the jigsaw method include the growth of self-control, self-management, ambition, independence, and social interaction. Jigsaw was also found to reduce intimidation in the classroom, which inhibits learning and leads to introverted student behavior. The academic benefits of jigsaw include improved reading abilities, systematic reproduction of knowledge, the improved ability to make conclusions, and summarizing.

Students in the jigsaw classrooms demonstrated improved knowledge as well as improved ability to apply that knowledge when compared with students in traditional classes. Students were not afraid to ask questions or to scrutinize presented information when they were able to ask for and get an explanation of something from a peer.

Classroom Applications

The jigsaw technique operates in six steps:

1. Separate a new part of the curriculum into several major sections. Each section will be focused on by a so-called "expert group" as described in Step 4.

2. Split a class of 25 students into 5 groups of 5 students each. These groups are the so-called base groups. (The groups should be heterogeneous in gender, cultural background, and achievement levels.)

3. Every member of the base group selects or is assigned one of the major sections. For example, one member might focus on the section on fractions, another might focus on the section on decimals, another might focus on the section on percentages, and so forth. If the number of group members exceeds the number of sections, two students can focus on the same section.

4. The base groups temporarily divide up so that each student can join a new group to become an "expert" on her or his topic. All the students focusing on fractions will be in one group, all the students focusing on decimals will be in another group, and so on. These students work together in temporary groups called *expert groups*. There the students acquire the knowledge about their topic and discuss how to teach it to students in their base groups.

5. Students return to their base groups and serve as the expert for their topics. Everyone then takes a turn teaching what he or she learned about to the members of his or her base group.

6. A written test is given to the entire class.

In Steps 4 and 5, students get an opportunity to discuss and exchange knowledge. Step 6 gives the teacher an opportunity to check the quality of students' work—to see what and how much the students learned from each other. One of the advantages of this method of cooperative learning is that in jigsaw there is always active learning going on and students do not become bored while passively listening to reports from other groups, as sometimes happens with the Johnson and Johnson "Learning Together" method.

Jigsaw can be used to teach a series of unrelated skills such as factoring, reducing or simplifying algebraic fractions, as well as topics that could tie together, such as word problems.

Precautions and Possible Pitfalls

While students teach members of their base groups in Step 5, teachers are frequently tempted to join in the discussions and advise students how to best teach the subject to their base group. This type of teacher intervention prevents the social and intellectual benefits of jigsaw. Although a teacher has to monitor groupwork to intervene when there are substantial mistakes in understanding the academic content, the teacher should not interfere with how students decide to teach this content to their peers.

SOURCES

Eppler, R., & Huber, G. L. (1990). Wissenswert im Team: Empirische Untersuchung von Effekten des Gruppen-Puzzles [Acquisition of knowledge in teams: An empirical study of effects of the jigsaw techniques]. *Psychologie in Erziehung und Unterricht, 37,* 172-178.

Aronson, E., Blaney, N., Stephan, C., Sikes, J., & Snapp, M. (1978). *The jigsaw classroom.* Beverly Hills, CA: Sage.

THE TIP (2.4)

 Do more than one thing at a time.

What the Research Says

Kounin's (1970) classic study of classroom management compared effective teachers with ineffective teachers. The effective teachers' classes did not have many problems whereas the ineffective teachers' classes were characterized by continuous disruption and chaos. By observing effective and ineffective teachers' classes, Kounin discovered that the major difference between them was in preventing problems rather than handling problems once they arose. One way teachers prevented problems was by "overlapping" activities, or supervising and keeping track of several activities at a time. To successfully overlap activities, effective teachers continuously monitored what was going on in the classroom.

Classroom Applications

There is an adage in the teaching world—the teacher needs to continuously move about the classroom and be omni-present. A critical time for the teacher's presence to be made known is at the beginning of a lesson. While students are putting homework problems on an overhead transparency or on the blackboard, the teacher is free to work with individual students. While a teacher or student is collecting homework assignments, the teacher can be introducing the class to the next topic by posing a problem or question to tap and review students' prior knowledge of the topic they will discuss next. While walking around the classroom discussing a topic, a teacher can glance at students' desks to check for homework or to make sure students are looking at the appropriate material. The teacher can also discuss how to solve a problem while walking around and making his or her presence known, making sure students do not misbehave.

Precautions and Possible Pitfalls

 The key thing to bear in mind is to not spread yourself too thin when assuming more than one responsibility at a time. In addition, don't move around the classroom so much that the movement becomes a distraction for students.

SOURCE

Kounin, J. (1970). *Discipline and group management in classrooms.* New York: Holt, Rinehart & Winston.

THE TIP (2.5)

 Avoid reacting emotionally when evaluating problematic situations in the classroom.

What the Research Says

An emotional reaction can prevent a teacher from objectively assessing a problematic situation. When a teacher displays a high level of emotional excitement, the teacher tends to evaluate situations more negatively than is objectively appropriate. This reaction is especially common when the teacher is very sensitive to the perception that students are not reacting satisfactorily to the teacher's demands. A cohort of 132 teachers participated in an investigation of how teachers evaluate problematic situations. The participants saw several videotapes with 1½- to 4-minute sequences that represented problematic situations. After every scene, teachers had to complete a questionnaire that asked for their observations, evaluations, estimations of the situation, emotions, and reactions. The extent of their emotional excitement was also requested.

Classroom Applications

Beware of creating vicious cycles! For example, teachers frequently penalize students who show a high degree of motor activity or conspicuous body language. Students may not be able to stop this activity immediately. When a teacher gets the impression that students are not reacting appropriately to his or her demand to stop an activity, the teacher then tends to evaluate the situation negatively and may react emotionally.

How to break the cycle:

- Sanction the student without causing embarrassment
- Be patient for a few seconds; students need time to realize just what you are asking of them and to change their behavior. (Careful! These seconds can take ages from your perspective.)
- Establish eye contact. In this way the student will get the impression that you mean it

- If it is necessary to repeat your demand, do it word-for-word as originally presented. Do not confront the student with what might appear to be a different demand or request. This could confuse the issue

Precautions and Possible Pitfalls

 To simultaneously appear both fair and strict, you must maintain self-control. If you suddenly become emotional, the student's behavior may worsen. By maintaining your equilibrium—not reacting emotionally in problematic situations—you can prevent the cycle from starting again.

SOURCE

Thienel, A. (1989). Der Einfluß der emotionalen Betroffenheit von Lehrern auf das differentielle Erleben einer Problemsituation [The influence of emotional excitement on the differential definitions of a problematic situation by teachers]. *Psychologie in Erziehung und Unterricht, 36,* 210-215.

THE TIP (2.6)

 If students do not follow your instructions, if their achievements do not fulfill your expectations, or both, the cause may not be students' incompetence. It could be a result of your self-overestimation.

What the Research Says

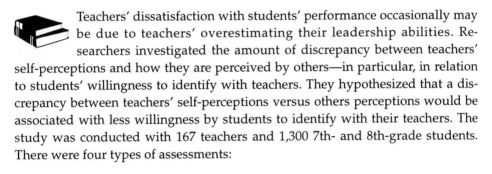 Teachers' dissatisfaction with students' performance occasionally may be due to teachers' overestimating their leadership abilities. Researchers investigated the amount of discrepancy between teachers' self-perceptions and how they are perceived by others—in particular, in relation to students' willingness to identify with teachers. They hypothesized that a discrepancy between teachers' self-perceptions versus others perceptions would be associated with less willingness by students to identify with their teachers. The study was conducted with 167 teachers and 1,300 7th- and 8th-grade students. There were four types of assessments:

1. Heads of the schools, where the teachers work, evaluated teachers' leadership by scaling 60 prescribed items. This was the "outside assessment," independent of students' feelings about the teachers.

2. Students completed a questionnaire asking for their impression of a teacher's leadership.

3. Students completed a questionnaire asking for their willingness to identify with their teachers in two different ways: on a social-personal level and on a performance-oriented level.

4. Teachers completed a questionnaire asking for their self-assessment of their leadership abilities.

The results showed the following:

- Students have a strong tendency to identify with the teachers who underestimate their capacity to make demands

- Teacher's self-overestimation (i.e., self-assessment versus outside assessment) makes students less willing to identify with teachers on a performance-oriented level and leads to personal rejection of the teacher

- A willingness to identify with teachers on a performance-oriented level is facilitated by teacher characteristics of patience, humor, and emotional safety

- A willingness to identify with teachers on a social-personal level is facilitated by teacher friendliness

- A willingness to identify with teachers on both levels increases when there is a high level of agreement between teacher's self-assessment and outside assessment or when the teacher's self-assessment is lower than the outside assessment

Classroom Applications

Assess the development of these teacher characteristics (patience, humor, emotional safety, and friendliness) in your personality! Ask friends. Watch yourself! Monitor your own demonstration of these characteristics during classroom instruction and other activities. Make specific changes to your own behavior as needed. Analyze your capacity to have high expectations for your students. If you feel that you lower your expectations to match student's willingness to complete assignments, try raising your expectations for a few weeks and check the results.

Consider the following possibilities for challenging students more:

- Make homework assignments more challenging
- Shorten the time allotted for written exercises
- Make students use correct grammar and vocabulary in their oral answers, written answers, or both
- Examine their notebooks

Consider having students work on an independent project resulting in a paper or report on a topic that is not part of the curriculum.

Precautions and Possible Pitfalls

Don't make the mistake of assuming students see you, and your expectations the same way you do. Try videotaping your class to allow you to observe and evaluate how students are reacting so that your self-assessment is more objective. When raising expectations, do *not* start with changes in grading student's work. Students, who are very sensitive about being treated unfairly, would see this as being unjust. Consequently, a sudden change in grading practices could backfire, making students more unwilling to identify with you both on a social-personal level and on a performance-oriented level. Make these changes gradually, in small increments. After 3 or 4 weeks, students are likely to accept the new higher standards.

SOURCE

Kessel, W. (1981). Selbstbild/Fremdbild: Differenz der Lehrer und Identifikationsbereitschaft der Schüler [Self-assessment and outside-assessment differences of teachers and student willingness to identify with teachers]. *Pädagogische Forschung, 22*(1), 533-560.

THE TIP (2.7)

 Make classroom activities flow smoothly.

What the Research Says

Kounin's (1970) classic study of classroom management compared effective teachers with ineffective teachers. The effective teachers' classes did not have many problems whereas continuous disruption and chaos characterized the ineffective teachers' classes. By observing effective and ineffective teachers' classes, Kounin discovered that the major difference between them was in preventing problems rather than handling problems once they arose. One way teachers prevented problems was by making sure students were not sitting around waiting for the next activity, but were engaged in meaningful work all the time. Effective teachers had smooth transitions between activities, they conducted activities at a flexible and reasonable pace, and their lessons involved a variety of activities.

Classroom Applications

The smooth beginning of a class is quite obviously an important aspect of an effective lesson. Rather than spending time having students copy their homework on the chalkboard at the beginning of a lesson, a smooth beginning would have them immediately presenting their work to the class on an overhead projector (or video monitor). Students should have their model solutions on a transparency when they enter the classroom (done the evening before as part of their homework) so that they can present their work without taking class time to copy it on a transparency.

Another example of a smooth transition is for the teacher to structure the order of topics to be presented in a logical way so that one comfortably leads into the next, or that one situation is an elaboration of its predecessor, and so on. Teachers should make sure transitions are smooth both in topics presented (content) and student activities (process). With the teacher conscious of these transitions, the likelihood of them happening smoothly is greatly increased.

Precautions and Possible Pitfalls

Be aware of the smoothness of a lesson's start. Student behavior and overall attitude will reflect the appropriateness of a lesson's level and tone. Be prepared to make modifications and adjust to the students' style (within reason, of course), and remember, there is no one best method. The "best method" may vary from class to class!

Some general suggestions include the following:

1. Avoid interrupting students while they are busy working.
2. Avoid returning to activities that have been treated as finished.
3. Avoid starting a new activity before finishing a preceding activity.
4. Avoid taking too much time when beginning a new activity. Slowing down can mean trouble.

SOURCE

Kounin, J. (1970). *Discipline and group management in classrooms.* New York: Holt, Rinehart & Winston

THE TIP (2.8)

 Give girls the same quantity and quality of teacher attention as boys.

What the Research Says

A study was conducted in 10 high school geometry classes in 2 school systems. One school system was in an urban-suburban community, with well-educated and relatively wealthy people. The other school system was in a lower class, less well-educated rural community. Each of the 10 mathematics teachers was observed 10 times for a total of 100 observations. The researchers used the Brophy Good Teacher-Child Dyadic Interaction System to study teacher-student contacts or interactions. They looked at and compared the quantity and quality of teachers' interactions with girls and boys. The results showed that teachers treated girls and boys differently in several ways, including responding to questions, the cognitive level or difficulty of questions asked, praise and criticism, encouragement, individual help, and conversation and joking. Generally, teachers acted in more positive ways with boys than with girls. Boys received more attention, more reinforcement, and more emotional support.

Classroom Applications

Teachers should make every effort to consciously and conscientiously encourage girls during regular classroom instruction. Boys should not be allowed to select the best seats in the classroom or to dominate students' responses. Teachers should take care not to show gender bias and should identify famous female mathematicians from the past and highlight their contributions to the development of mathematics. There are a number of books available from professional organizations and commercial publishers that address the issue of women in mathematics. For example, from the National Council of Teachers of Mathematics (1906 Association Drive, Reston, VA 20191-1593) the following titles are available: *Celebrating Women in Mathematics and Science, Multicultural and Gender Equity in the Mathematics Classroom, New Directions for Equity in Mathematics Education,* and *Reaching All Students With Mathematics.*

Precautions and Possible Pitfalls

⚠ Teachers should make this inclusion of gender issues a natural part of the instructional program and not merely an add-on. The latter would seem obvious and unnatural and would defeat the purpose. Be aware that cultural influences often negatively affect girls' attitudes about and their capabilities and performances in mathematics.

SOURCE

Becker, J. R. (1981). Differential treatment of females and males in mathematics classes. *Journal for Research in Mathematics Education, 12*(1) 40-53.

THE TIP (2.9)

 Make special efforts to encourage girls to study mathematics.

What the Research Says

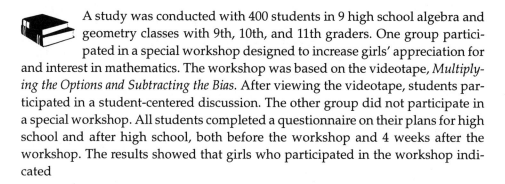 A study was conducted with 400 students in 9 high school algebra and geometry classes with 9th, 10th, and 11th graders. One group participated in a special workshop designed to increase girls' appreciation for and interest in mathematics. The workshop was based on the videotape, *Multiplying the Options and Subtracting the Bias*. After viewing the videotape, students participated in a student-centered discussion. The other group did not participate in a special workshop. All students completed a questionnaire on their plans for high school and after high school, both before the workshop and 4 weeks after the workshop. The results showed that girls who participated in the workshop indicated

- They were going to study more mathematics both during and after high school

- They actually did enroll in more mathematics courses in high school

- They changed in their perception of the usefulness of mathematics for their future lives

- Their plans to study mathematics were significantly related to changes in this perception.

Classroom Applications

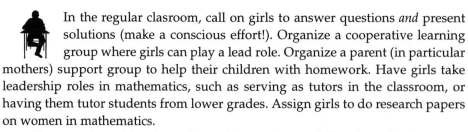 In the regular clasroom, call on girls to answer questions *and* present solutions (make a conscious effort!). Organize a cooperative learning group where girls can play a lead role. Organize a parent (in particular mothers) support group to help their children with homework. Have girls take leadership roles in mathematics, such as serving as tutors in the classroom, or having them tutor students from lower grades. Assign girls to do research papers on women in mathematics.

There are lots of female mathematicians who would be pleased to come to a secondary school to either give a talk to a class on career options or who would give a content talk to a mathematics class. A list of such persons can be obtained from the Mathematical Association of America, or from the American Mathematics Society. Further information can be found in the numerous publications from these organizations and from commercial publishers. There are a number of books available from professional organizations and commercial publishers that focus on women in mathematics. The National Council of Teachers of Mathematics (1906 Association Drive, Reston, VA 20191-1593) offers the following suggestions: *Celebrating Women in Mathematics and Science, Multicultural and Gender Equity in the Mathematics Classroom, New Directions for Equity in Mathematics Education,* and *Reaching All Students With Mathematics.*

Precautions and Possible Pitfalls

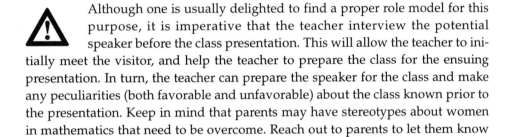 Although one is usually delighted to find a proper role model for this purpose, it is imperative that the teacher interview the potential speaker before the class presentation. This will allow the teacher to initially meet the visitor, and help the teacher to prepare the class for the ensuing presentation. In turn, the teacher can prepare the speaker for the class and make any peculiarities (both favorable and unfavorable) about the class known prior to the presentation. Keep in mind that parents may have stereotypes about women in mathematics that need to be overcome. Reach out to parents to let them know girls can be as successful as boys in mathematics—both in their schoolwork and in careers.

SOURCE

Fennema, E., Wolleat, P. L., Pedro, J. D., & Becker, A. D. (1981). Increasing women's participation in mathematics: An intervention study. *Journal for Research in Mathematics Education, 12*(1), 3–14.

THE TIP (2.10)

 Make multicultural connections in mathematics.

What the Research Says

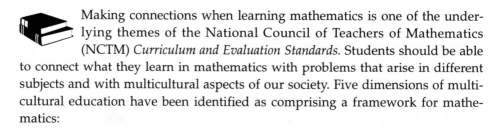 Making connections when learning mathematics is one of the under-lying themes of the National Council of Teachers of Mathematics (NCTM) *Curriculum and Evaluation Standards*. Students should be able to connect what they learn in mathematics with problems that arise in different subjects and with multicultural aspects of our society. Five dimensions of multi-cultural education have been identified as comprising a framework for mathematics:

- *Integrate content* reflecting diversity when teaching key points
- *Construct knowledge* so students understand how peoples' points of view within a discipline influence the conclusions they reach in a discipline
- *Reduce prejudice* so students develop positive attitudes toward different groups of people
- *Use instructional techniques* that will promote achievement from diverse groups of students
- *Modify the school culture* to ensure that people from diverse groups are empowered and have educational equality

Classroom Applications

 Examples of how to apply the five multicultural dimensions to mathematics include the following:

1. *Integrate content* so that the history of mathematics includes contributions of mathematicians from many cultures and ethnicities, and is not Eurocentric. Examples: Teach students about Benjamin Banneker, an African American creator of mathematical puzzles; teach them about proofs of the Pythagorean Theorem from China, India, and Babylon.

2. *Construct knowledge* so students see the universal nature of the mathematical components of measuring, counting, locating, and designing.

3. *Reduce prejudice* by using mathematics (statistical data) to eliminate stereotypes. Examples: Show there are more whites than blacks who are on welfare; teach the economic value of recycling bottles and cans through the story, *The Black Snowman* (Mendez, 1989).

4. *Use instructional techniques* that motivate students and facilitate mutual respect for culture. Example: Teach students about positive and negative numbers through traveling on a subway and identifying subway stops after and before students board the train.

5. *Modify the school culture* so students from diverse cultures are grouped together, can participate in extracurricular activities, and so teachers have high expectations for success from all students, regardless of diverse cultural backgrounds. Examples: After writing a brief report on one of the people identified in example 1 (p. 122), have students role-play these famous mathematicians. In addition, cooperative learning has been demonstrated to promote mutual respect of students from culturally different backgrounds.

Precautions and Possible Pitfalls

 Make sure that multicultural aspects of lessons are not done in a patronizing manner.

SOURCES

Banks, J. A. (1994). Transforming the mainstream curriculum. *Educational Leadership, 51*(8), 4-8.

Bishop, A. (1988). Mathematics education in its cultural context. *Educational Studies in Mathematics, 19*, 179-191.

Mendez, P. (1989). *The black snowman.* New York: Scholastic Press.

Moses, R., Kamii, M., Swap, S., & Howard, J. (1989). The Algebra Project: Organizing in the spirit of Ella. *Harvard Educational Review, 59*(4), 423-443.

Strutchens, M. (1995). *Multicultural mathematics: A more inclusive mathematics.* Columbus, OH: ERIC Digest, Clearinghouse for Science, Mathematics, and Environmental Education. (ERIC Document Reproduction Service No. ED 380 295)

THE TIP (2.11)

 Reflect on your assessment of girls' and boys' achievements based on their oral communications.

What the Research Says

Teachers often are unaware of their unconscious discrimination based on gender and social interaction variables. Social interaction variables, such as those that occur in oral communications, influence teacher's judgment of student's achievements. In general, boys receive more confirmation and reinforcement from teachers than girls. This is especially true for female teachers. In a study with 11 classes, Grades 5 to 12, 40 lessons were videotaped. These lessons were analyzed for the connection between social phenomena and assessments of students. Researchers analyzed the way students represented their knowledge and understanding during mathematics lessons by looking at oral interactions between the students with each other as well as with the teacher. The researchers investigated whether teachers' and students' interpretations or actions in mathematics differed as a function of gender.

Examples of oral interactions studied include tone of voice—whether it sounds undecided, if the voice is raised, if words are stressed when pronounced, whether there is a 4-second "wait time" pause, and if hands are raised or lowered. When a male student raised his voice at the end of a communication, it functioned as an invitation for the female teacher to give a verbal or nonverbal confirmation to the boy so he could continue speaking. The verbal interaction continued with the student speaking and the teacher paraphrasing or echoing (repeating exactly) what the student said. The teacher even completed the boy's statement in a way that produced the correct answer. She gave another boy hints or directions that moved him closer to the correct answer. The results showed that students usually wait for signals from the teacher inviting them to continue speaking or not. Without the teacher's signal, students are unlikely to continue speaking. Girls tend to receive fewer signals to continue speaking than boys and are also less likely to get hints or directions from the teacher moving them to the correct answer. Teachers do this unconsciously, without deliberate intent or self-awareness.

Classroom Applications

Use self-control to make sure you don't complete students' sentences and thereby conceal a student's lack of knowledge or understanding. Instead, you can call on another student to complete the answer. Do *not* fall for students' unconscious social interaction cues, such as raising one's voice at the end of a communication. A teacher takes this automatically as an invitation to confirm, reinforce, or complete what the student has said.

Precautions and Possible Pitfalls

If you try everything to prevent discrimination in treatment between boys and girls, they might actually interpret this as unfair, because from their experience the equal treatment of boys and girls deviates from the norm! Until you change your behavior, students may not have noticed the unequal treatment of boys and girls because it is so common. The change may alter their habits and arouse their perception of how they are treated. Then the other sex might feel there is gender-based discrimination!

SOURCE

Jungwirth, H. (1991). Mathematische Kompetenz als soziales Phänomen [Mathematical competence seen as a social phenomenon]. *Mathematica Didactica, 14*(1), 30-45.

THE TIP (2.12)

 Take into consideration how students view successful teachers, and how this differs for girls and boys.

What the Research Says

 Girls are more critical of a teacher's appearance and behavior than are boys. Female teachers were evaluated more frequently than male teachers as unfair and too soft. Female teachers, however, were regarded as less nervous, less disorderly, and are more punctual than male teachers. Besides, female teachers do not make excessive demands on students and they smoke less! Female teachers get thoroughly evaluated by students in their social behavior and their dress. Male teachers were evaluated more critically in their politics and philosophy.

Participants were 40 male and female teachers and their students from Grades 5 to 10.

The experiment consisted of four phases:

Phase 1: A questionnaire that asked students for their view of the characteristics of effective teachers

Phase 2: Observation of teachers' actions during lessons

Phase 3: Analyses of teachers' personalities

Phase 4: Procedures to improve or stabilize favorable teacher characteristics

The results showed that cheerfulness was the characteristic that was cited by students of all age groups. Most student views of the characteristics of effective teachers changed with the students' age. For example, being good at explaining facts was considered an effective characteristic by 34% of 8th graders, 41% of 9th graders, and 50% of 10th graders. The most frequent negative characteristics identified were being nervous, making excessive demands, being disorderly, being late, and smoking.

Thirteen positive characteristics of effective teachers were identified:

1. Having good methodology
2. Identifying the aim of a lesson
3. Dividing tasks into parts
4. Supplying or demanding summaries of a lesson
5. Providing tasks with a high degree of difficulty

6. Getting students to think automatically

7. Stimulating comments

8. Involving students actively in learning

9. Refraining from making discouraging comments when students make mistakes

10. Focusing on the essential points

11. Giving students individual help or making individual demands

12. Giving varied assessments

13. Evaluating a student's personality from a positive perspective

Classroom Applications

Teachers should be aware of the characteristics their students consider important. Female teachers are likely to find it harder to get students' respect than male teachers. Because cheerfulness was considered important by students of all ages, teachers could benefit from making a deliberate attempt to be more cheerful, if they are not cheerful already. The mathematics teacher can influence the way in which students see them by delving into the field often referred to as "recreational mathematics." This will garner greater teacher enthusiasm because of the novelty of the topics, and will then enable the teacher to stand out from among the rest of the teachers.

Precautions and Possible Pitfalls

Being polite, always speaking gently to the students, encouraging them, and so forth is something that students expect from female teachers, but this alone does not work. A male teacher should not rely only on his professional knowledge. Although professional knowledge is important, there are other aspects of conducting a lesson that are important.

SOURCE

Grassel, H. (1968). *Probleme und Ergebnisse von Untersuchungen der Lehrertätigkeit und Lehrerwirksamkeit* [Problems and results of investigations regarding teacher's activity and teacher's effectiveness]. Rostock, Germany: Studie des Wissenschaftsbereichs Pädagogische Psychologie der Universität Rostock.

THE TIP (2.13)

☑ Do not assume that students accept responsibility for or agree with their bad grades on tests.

What the Research Says

 Teachers should be aware that students often just partially accept a teacher's grades. Many students overestimate their achievements and expect better grades than they get. When giving reasons for their good and bad grades on reports and tests, students explained their good grades by the efforts they made. In contrast, when explaining why they got bad grades, students attributed their bad grades on tests to "tough luck," whereas they explained their bad grades on reports to their "lack of effort." A study was conducted with 146 students aged 15 to 18. Students were asked to evaluate the responsibility for their grades from four sources: (a) students themselves, (b) teacher, (c) other students, (d) the situation.

Students also rated their satisfaction with their grades and their perception of the fairness of the grade on a 4-point scale. Satisfaction was measured by student responses to, "Because of my achievements I deserved a better grade." Fairness was measured by having them respond to, "In comparison with the other students my grade is not fair." The results showed that students' expectations for their grades were consistent with the teacher's expectations 66% of the time, whereas 23% of the time they expected a better grade, and 11% of the time they expected a worse grade. When students received grades that were lower than they expected, they were dissatisfied with their grades and judged them to be unfair. Finally, the results showed that students usually ascribed responsibility for their grades to someone other than themselves.

Classroom Applications

Just as it is important for a teacher to praise or make specific comments about a student's good grades, the teacher should make specific comments about the reason for students' bad grades. Otherwise the student is likely to externalize responsibility for his or her bad grades, explaining them by too little practice, too difficult tests, not enough time, and so forth. The teacher should give detailed feedback regarding a student's weaknesses, but in a constructive manner. Mathematics teachers sometimes forget to do this. They expect the knowledge that an answer is wrong or right to be sufficient. Far from it! Students who get bad grades are attempting to justify their bad grades with external circumstances to preserve their self-respect.

Precautions and Possible Pitfalls

 Do not embarrass or humiliate your students! To help preserve their self-respect, it is recommended that you give students feedback on their bad grades in private—not in front of the whole class. Written notes or personal comments after the lesson are much more helpful. Recognize that students who consistently perform at a lower level are likely to expect better grades than they actually get. Consequently, such a student's reaction is usually one of disappointment and the student is likely to be sensitive about it. In such situations, many students tend to feign indifference or amusement about bad grades. Do not be misled or discouraged by this or take it personally. Continue to provide feedback constructively about the reasons for bad grades.

SOURCE

Allmer, H. (1982). Selbstverantwortlichkeit und Schülerzufriedenheit nach erwarteter und unerwarteter Leistungsbewertung [Self-responsibility and satisfaction of pupils after expected and unexpected performance evaluation]. *Psychologie in Erziehung und Unterricht, 29,* 321-327.

THE TIP (2.14)

☑ Use classwide peer tutoring to help your students learn, whether or not they have learning disabilities.

What the Research Says

 A whole classroom of students helping other students has been found to be an efficient and effective method of enhancing achievement. Twenty teachers participated in a study of classwide peer tutoring with 40 classrooms in elementary and middle schools. Half of the schools implemented classwide peer tutoring programs and half did not. Both urban and suburban schools participated in the study. Students came from diverse backgrounds, both culturally and linguistically. There were three different categories of students: average achievers, low achievers without learning disabilities, and low achievers with learning disabilities.

The peer tutoring programs were conducted 3 days a week, for 35 minutes a day, for 15 weeks. Stronger students were paired with weaker students. Teachers reviewed each pair to ensure they were socially compatible. In all pairs, students took turns serving in the roles of tutor and tutee. Student pairs worked together for 4 weeks; then teachers arranged new pairings. Teachers received training on how to train their students to be tutors. Tutor training included teaching students how to correct each other's errors. Achievement tests were administered before and after the peer-tutoring program. Regardless of whether students were average achievers or low achievers, with or without learning disabilities, students in the peer tutoring classrooms achieved at higher levels than those in the classrooms without classwide peer tutoring.

Classroom Applications

There are many areas in mathematics that lend themselves to a peer-tutoring program. When there is a skill to be learned and all one needs is experience with success (i.e., drill with immediate feedback), peer tutoring could provide an efficient way to monitor and support a student trying to master the skill. Perhaps a student has difficulty with factoring—part of his or her problem is recognizing which type of factoring is called for and when more than one type of factoring may be used, the situation becomes doubly confusing.

Here, a peer tutor, under the guidance of a teacher, can be quite beneficial. A student who has difficulty doing geometric theorem proofs could find a peer tutor a genuine asset. In addition, the tutor, by explaining the proof to the student, is also provided with an opportunity to strengthen his or her own understanding of the concept of proof (a higher-order thinking skill), and with the role of proof in mathematics. Thus, there is often a mutual benefit to a peer-tutoring program.

Precautions and Possible Pitfalls

 A tutor-training program offered by the teacher must precede peer tutoring. Tutors must be given some instruction on how to conduct the sessions, what sort of difficulties to look for on the part of the tutee, and what points to stress in the sessions (based on the teacher's assessment of the class). Any individual difficulties on the part of the tutees should be mentioned to the tutor prior to the sessions. Tutors should be taught to guide student learning, and not merely solve problems for students. Students with severe learning disabilities may be too disruptive to benefit from classwide peer tutoring, unless the tutors first receive individualized instruction from learning disabilities specialists.

SOURCE

Fuchs, D., Fuchs, L., Mathes, P. G., & Simmons, D. (1997). Peer-assisted learning strategies: Making classrooms more responsive to diversity. *American Educational Research Journal, 34*(1), 174-206.

THE TIP (2.15)

 Use group problem solving to stimulate students to apply mathematical thinking skills.

What the Research Says

Students interacting with other students when solving problems in a group stimulates basic (cognitive) and higher-level (metacognitive) mathematical thinking skills. A study was conducted with 27 average-ability seventh graders in an urban school. A total of 73 problem-solving behaviors were examined for each student. One week before the study, students were put into heterogeneous groups so they could become familiar with how to work in groups and with the members of their groups. Heterogeneous groups were balanced for ability, gender, race, and ethnicity. No time limit was given for groups to solve the assigned problem. Groups were videotaped as they solved the problem. Working in groups to solve the problem, students engaged in the following types of mathematical thinking:

- Reading the problem (basic)
- Understanding the problem (higher level)
- Analyzing the problem (higher level)
- Planning an approach to solve the problem (higher level)
- Exploring a problem-solving approach to see whether or not it works (basic and higher level)
- Implementing the plan for solving the problem (basic and higher level)
- Verifying the final solution (basic and higher level)
- Listening to and watching other students during the problem-solving process

The greatest percentage of higher-level mathematical thinking occurred while students were exploring a solution; the second greatest percentage occurred as students were trying to understand the problem. The highest percentage of basic mathematical thinking occurred during exploration; the second highest occurred while students were reading the problem.

Classroom Applications

Carefully select problems that will stimulate use of mathematical thinking and problem solving when preparing for group activities. Observe groups as they are working and intervene only as needed. After most groups seem to have finished, call the groups back together and have them describe their problem-solving processes and answers. Call attention to the mathematical thinking and problem-solving processes they were used, both when conferring with individual groups, and when after all groups have been called back together. Explicitly use the eight concepts described here when discussing problem solving to increase students' awareness of how they are thinking mathematically and how they are solving problems. Don't set rigid time limits for solving the problem. Let each group work at its own pace.

Precautions and Possible Pitfalls

Not all groups will behave in the same way. Some groups will not engage in all eight of the problem-solving behavior categories described, and those that do may engage in them in varying degrees. In addition, not all groups will be successful in solving a given problem. If one group (or more) finishes before the others, make sure you have a follow-up task ready so students can extend their thinking rather than get bored and waste time waiting for the others to finish.

SOURCE

Artzt, A., & Armour-Thomas, E. (1992). Development of a cognitive-metacognitive framework for protocol analysis of group problem solving in mathematics. *Cognition and Instruction, 9*(2), 137-175.

THE TIP (2.16)

 Call on students more frequently to promote their achievement.

What the Research Says

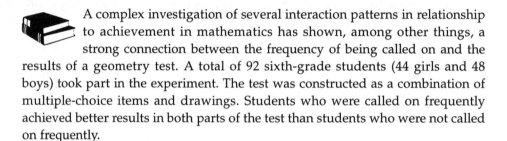 A complex investigation of several interaction patterns in relationship to achievement in mathematics has shown, among other things, a strong connection between the frequency of being called on and the results of a geometry test. A total of 92 sixth-grade students (44 girls and 48 boys) took part in the experiment. The test was constructed as a combination of multiple-choice items and drawings. Students who were called on frequently achieved better results in both parts of the test than students who were not called on frequently.

Classroom Applications

 If you ask a question or assign a task and only a few students raise their hands, who should you call on?

(a) The student who raised his or her hand at first?

(b) The student who raised his or her hand first time this day?

(c) The student who is involved in the lesson most actively?

(d) The student who guarantees a correct answer?

(e) The student who does not raise his or her hand, but who is known to be intelligent?

(f) The student who is too reserved or anxious to raise his or her hand?

(g) The student who seems to be inattentive?

The list could be continued almost indefinitely. This example illustrates that a teacher's decision about who he or she will call on is not easy, and the teacher has to make this decision in a very short amount of time. It is impossible to always make the right decision. Whenever you call on one student, other students may feel neglected. You can, however, pay attention to and take control of the situation, making sure that you do not concentrate most of your attention on just a few students. Research has shown that teachers tend to pay more attention to students who are known as intelligent, such as those in (a), (c), (d), and (e) in the list presented. Although students with learning weaknesses often give a wrong answer or no answer, it is necessary to invest the time in calling on them. Otherwise, their chance to achieve is reduced even further.

Precautions and Possible Pitfalls

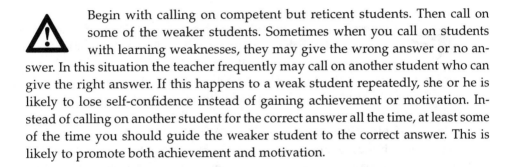 Begin with calling on competent but reticent students. Then call on some of the weaker students. Sometimes when you call on students with learning weaknesses, they may give the wrong answer or no answer. In this situation the teacher frequently may call on another student who can give the right answer. If this happens to a weak student repeatedly, she or he is likely to lose self-confidence instead of gaining achievement or motivation. Instead of calling on another student for the correct answer all the time, at least some of the time you should guide the weaker student to the correct answer. This is likely to promote both achievement and motivation.

SOURCE

Heymann, H. -W. (1978). *Lehr-Lern Prozesse im Mathematikunterricht. Analysen im Bereich der Orientierungsstufe* [Processes of teaching and learning in mathematics classes]. Stuttgart, Germany: Klett-Cotta.

THE TIP (2.17)

 Reflect on your own behavior and consider whether students' aggressive behavior is a subtle reaction to your own aggressiveness!

What the Research Says

Aggressiveness in students sometimes is an indirect reflection of teachers' aggressive behavior. Research has shown that students react to teacher's aggressiveness with aggressiveness of their own. One significant point was that the teacher has to behave aggressively a certain number of times before the student would respond with aggressiveness. Another significant point was that, contrary to the researchers' predictions, the students' aggressive behavior would differ from the teacher's. A teacher's verbal aggressiveness tends to produce physical aggressiveness in students while a teacher's physical aggressiveness tends to produce verbal aggressiveness in students. Research on the interaction between students and teachers was conducted with three 8th-grade classes over a period of about 2 months. After that time, 33 students who showed aggressive behavior were selected. These 33 students formed the actual data sample for this study. Aggressiveness was defined as follows:

Category	Examples
Indirect verbal aggression	Laugh at, deride
Direct verbal aggression	Forbid, threaten, command, demand (put under pressure to affect someone), curse, scream, abuse (irrational emotion and negative affects), destructive criticism, dismissive reaction on suggestions (rational directed refusal)
Indirect physical aggression	Pursue, physically threaten, take something away
Direct physical aggression	Beat, wrestle, kick, push, pull

Classroom Applications

 Often, teachers react to a lack of discipline in the class with verbal aggressiveness. In such situations, teachers may scream at students, make strong demands, command students, or threaten them with tests. Such actions usually tend to fail. Instead of producing the desired discipline, student's behavior becomes worse. The teacher's aggressiveness stimulates a very subtle aggressive reaction from students. In addition, mathematics teachers often speak very rapidly, especially in question-answer sequences, which involve few or short words. This speed of communication can appear as verbal aggressiveness, especially if the teacher does not get the correct answers. In such cases, the teacher often tries to drive students to the right answer by asking more and more questions, which they formulate in rapid succession. This is a form of verbal aggressiveness. Teachers seldom recognize their own responsibility for students' aggressive behaviors. Research has shown, however, that students act in reciprocal, but not identical aggressive ways. Although a teacher can be understandably excited in some classroom situations, it is important to avoid using an aggressive tone of voice or insulting words (including sarcasm). Speak calmly! Take the time to find the right words.

Precautions and Possible Pitfalls

Although it is recommended that teachers react to a student's physical aggressiveness with calmness, this does not mean teachers are supposed to react in a friendly manner. A friendly reaction by the teacher in such a tense situation with students would be interpreted as sign of the teacher's insecurity, which would reinforce the student's misbehavior. Acting calmly means being firm, reserved, and polite.

SOURCE

Knapp, A. (1984). Auswirkungen aggressiven Verhaltens von Lehrern auf das Verhalten ihrer Schüler [The effects of teacher's aggressive behavior on their student's behavior]. *Psychologie in Erziehung und Unterricht, 31,* 288-291.

THE TIP (2.18)

 Have "eyes in the back of your head" so you notice misbehavior at an early stage.

What the Research Says

In Kounin's (1970) classic study of classroom management, the major difference between effective and ineffective teachers' classrooms was in preventing problems rather than handling problems after they arose, thus causing continuous disruption and chaos. By observing effective and ineffective teachers' classes, Kounin discovered that one way teachers prevented problems was by "withitness." This was the teachers' ability to be aware of what individual students were doing at all times. They were aware of what was going on in the classroom, even while they were working with a few individual students. These teachers were described as having "eyes in the back of their heads." With this alertness, teachers were able to prevent minor problems from becoming major problems and, when a problem did arise, they were able to pinpoint the cause or culprit and put a quick end to the disturbance. This enabled the teacher to expeditiously deal with the problem at hand and effectively avoid its exacerbation and recurrence.

Classroom Applications

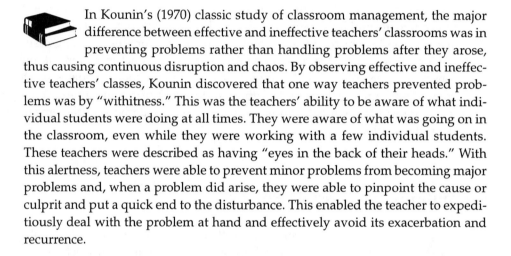 There are numerous "tricks" that teachers can use to achieve "withitness":

Remember that the spot from which you address the class is the temporary "front of the room." Constantly move around the classroom; don't stand in one spot. This allows most of the class to be at the front of the room at least for a part of the lesson, or arrange the class in a semicircle so most, or all, students can be in the front during a lesson.

Talk to the class even as you write. This will remind them that your thoughts are still on them and not on the board work. Don't turn your back to the class, except for very brief intervals.

Don't talk to one student while ignoring the rest of the class. If you speak to one student, do so while looking at the rest of the class at the same time.

Don't always call on volunteer responses to teacher questions. Call on those students who tend to look away from the teacher as soon as a question is asked.

Frequently make eye contact with students who tend to cause disruptions so they know you're paying attention to them.

While working with one cooperative learning group, look around the classroom to see how other groups are working. Make comments as necessary. Let them know that although you are working with one group, you are not ignoring what the other groups are doing.

Precautions and Possible Pitfalls

 The way to be "withit" is an individual phenomenon. A teacher must do what is consistent with his or her personality. To do otherwise would be counterproductive because students are very adept at identifying unnatural behavior. Remember that there is no perfect universal solution to maintaining proper class control. The suggestions presented here are merely ones that may be modified to meet individual personalities and strengths.

SOURCE

Kounin, J. (1970). *Discipline and group management in classrooms.* New York: Holt, Rinehart & Winston.

CHAPTER THREE

Beyond the Classroom

THE TIP (3.1)

 Use school fundraising projects, such as students selling candy, as the basis of mathematics lessons.

What the Research Says

Fundraising activities, such as students selling candy to raise money for a trip or for special equipment, can be used as the basis of meaningful mathematics learning. One study examined how children develop and use mathematical knowledge through their experiences selling candy. This research showed that the hands-on experience of acting as a sales person helped students to learn and understand important mathematical knowledge that they were later able to apply to working on school problems.

Classroom Applications

If there is a school store in your school, it would be a good idea to make contact with the store manager and offer your class's services to do the accounting for the operation. This would require getting all the purchasing and sales information about the store and having the class decide how to manage the information. If there is no school store, you might start one or get the principal's permission to undertake a project of fundraising. Funds so generated may be used for school improvements or to purchase important equipment for the school, such as band uniforms or computers. Students could also combine mathematics with social studies content by raising funds to be contributed to a local charity for homeless people. Once the project has been approved and the plan set, let students calculate the cost of doing business, the price of the items to be sold and the anticipated profit based on specific sales results.

More sophisticated mathematics (or higher-order thinking skills) can be used by having students estimate how much money they would generate if they offered different discount rates on the items they were selling. Students could compare the relative benefits of conducting different types of fundraising events, such as bake sales versus the sale of tee shirts. In addition, they could make projections for next year's fundraising target based on current data. Finally, they could compare the success of school fundraising strategies with those of nonschool fundraisers, such as local churches sponsoring benefit dinners or raffle ticket sales.

Precautions and Possible Pitfalls

 Care must be taken to ensure that the activities undertaken support the mathematics program and that the "business" doesn't take on a life of its own, where the main (original) purpose of motivating and exciting students about mathematics gets lost.

SOURCE

Saxe, G. B. (1988). Selling candy and math learning. *Educational Researcher, 17*(6), 14-21.

THE TIP (3.2)

 Use homework as a way of delving more deeply into important mathematical concepts and skills.

What the Research Says

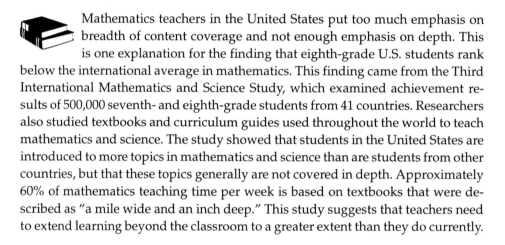 Mathematics teachers in the United States put too much emphasis on breadth of content coverage and not enough emphasis on depth. This is one explanation for the finding that eighth-grade U.S. students rank below the international average in mathematics. This finding came from the Third International Mathematics and Science Study, which examined achievement results of 500,000 seventh- and eighth-grade students from 41 countries. Researchers also studied textbooks and curriculum guides used throughout the world to teach mathematics and science. The study showed that students in the United States are introduced to more topics in mathematics and science than are students from other countries, but that these topics generally are not covered in depth. Approximately 60% of mathematics teaching time per week is based on textbooks that were described as "a mile wide and an inch deep." This study suggests that teachers need to extend learning beyond the classroom to a greater extent than they do currently.

Classroom Applications

Plan homework assignments as carefully as you plan your classroom lessons. Both the quality of the homework assignments and the amount of time students spend doing their homework are important for improving achievement in mathematics. An assignment that merely asks students to do, for example, Exercises 2-20 (even numbers only) on a specific textbook page is one that does not show much thought. It is not an activity that enables the student to deepen a knowledge of the concepts presented. Rather, it simply provides practice with a skill. Because classroom time is limited, use homework to give students more experience understanding and applying important concepts and skills.

Precautions and Possible Pitfalls

 Don't fall into the rut of making the same homework assignments year after year for class after class. Tailor your homework assignments to the needs of the specific students and classes. Take into consideration how much time students were actively engaged in classroom learning, and how much time was spent on classroom management or other administrative tasks.

SOURCES

Checkley, K. (1997). International mathematics and science study calls for depth, not breadth. *Education Update, 39*(1), 1, 3, 8.

Schmidt, W. (1997). *A splintered vision: An investigation of U.S. science and mathematics education.* Hingham, MA: Kluwer.

THE TIP (3.3)

 Use homework assignments as opportunities for students to get practice and feedback on applying their mathematical knowledge and skills.

What the Research Says

Giving students numerous and well-designed homework problems to solve can help students improve their performance in mathematics by giving them opportunities for practice and feedback. Research indicates that many hours of practice are needed for students to be successful in mathematics. In a review of the literature of the cognitive aspects of problem solving, the following benefits of practice with feedback were identified:

- The recollection of facts and concepts
- The recognition of patterns
- The recollection of strategies or procedures that can operate on patterns
- The use of strategies or procedures automatically
- The facilitation of work with problems presented in unfamiliar forms
- The analysis and identification of errors
- The development of problem-solving skills
- The development of important cognitive skills that cannot be explicitly taught
- The improvement of performance in creative problem solving, including solving problems that require "insight" or productive thinking rather than reproductive thinking
- The improved speed of problem solving

Classroom Applications

 Homework assignments must be carefully designed. The exercises should be selected to provide a balance of problems solvable by all students, problems solvable by most students, and a few problems that may be given as a challenge for the better, or more motivated students. Teachers should assign homework exercises that reflect a mixture of topics taught, thereby putting the various topics into the larger context of the course. They might wish to spiral back over previously taught material so students get a sense of "context." They may also wish to foreshadow some topics by giving them a guided series of questions that lead directly to the next topic. For example, the teacher planning to introduce the proof of the Pythagorean Theorem on one day, may wish to have students identify the three mean proportional relationships involving the segments of the hypotenuse of a right triangle, when the altitude is drawn on the hypotenuse. The resulting proportions lead directly to one of the common proofs of the Pythagorean Theorem. You may wish to consult E. S. Loomis's (1968) classic book, *The Pythagorean Proposition*, for other proofs of this famous theorem, some of which could also be used to foreshadow, via a homework exercise, the proof of this theorem. For a more detailed discussion of how homework can be assigned and reviewed in class, see *Teaching Secondary School Mathematics: Techniques and Enrichment Units* by A. S. Posamentier and N. Stepelman (1998).

Precautions and Possible Pitfalls

Avoid the common teaching practice in mathematics of having students focus on the course topic by topic. Caution should be used for any homework assignment not to assign exercises that are merely repetitions of each other, but with different numbers used. This is not only extremely boring, but serves no purpose in the learning process. Often, students do these by rote methods where *not* thinking is involved.

SOURCES

Frederiksen, N. (1984). Implications of cognitive theory for instruction in problem solving. *Review of Educational Research, 54*(3), 363-407.

Loomis, E. S. (1968). *The Pythagorean proposition*. Reston, VA: National Council of Teachers of Mathematics.

THE TIP (3.4)

 Select and carefully structure homework assignments so that they require the development of mathematical thinking and reasoning. Anticipate changes that might occur while students are working at home.

What the Research Says

The mathematical tasks that teachers use have a major impact on the kinds of mathematical thinking that students do. For example, perfunctory questions that require only yes/no answers do not expand higher-level mathematical thinking, whereas thought-provoking tasks do. Research has shown also that the tasks set up by the teacher may change, while students are working on them, due to complex factors in the environment. Such changes have been demonstrated to occur in the classroom and similar changes could occur at home. A sample of 144 mathematical tasks was analyzed by the features of the tasks and by the cognitive demands required by students engaged in these tasks. Features of the tasks analyzed included communication requirements (e.g., produce mathematical explanations or justifications), number of solution strategies, and number and kind of representations. Cognitive demands analyzed included memorizing, using procedures with and without connections to concepts, and doing mathematics. Researchers observed teachers announcing the tasks to students (set up) and observed students working on them (implementation). Observations occurred in three teachers' classrooms at four project sites over a 3-year period, spanning sixth grade through eighth grade. Videotapes were made of the lessons to supplement observations. The results documented changes from set up to implementation in the cognitive demands, in the number of solution strategies, in the number and kind of representations, and in the communication requirements.

Classroom Applications

A good habit to nurture is to preview the homework assignment before the students work on it. In this way, students know exactly what is expected of them and where to place their emphasis at home. For example, if the homework assignment is to practice solving quadratic equations, the teacher might elicit from students the various types of equations they may face, as well as the types of solution methods expected of them. The teacher might also ask students what type of format they would use to make sure their thinking is headed in the right direction. Whenever possible, to promote the development of mathematical thinking and reasoning, teachers should elicit ideas and information from students instead of telling it to the students. If students aren't forthcoming with the appropriate information, then it is appropriate for the teacher to provide it and/or clarify ideas presented by students. It's a good idea to vary homework assignments nightly so students do not get into a rut—doing their assignments by rote instead of thinking about what they are doing and why. One possible assignment to stimulate mathematical thinking and reasoning could be to have students select a topic within an area of mathematics and research it for a presentation to the class. Students may also select a topic from the history of mathematics, such as how calculations were made in different periods of time, the significance of a particular mathematician's work, or the etymology of mathematical symbols or expressions. Such assignments should dovetail with regular classroom work.

Precautions and Possible Pitfalls

 Don't preview the homework assignment to the extent that it might take some of the "suspense" or excitement out of the assignment. It is, however, important for the teacher to prepare the class for the assignment.

SOURCE

Stein, M. K., Grover, B. W., & Henningsen, M. (1996). Building student capacity for mathematical thinking and reasoning: An analysis of mathematical tasks used in reform classrooms. *American Educational Research Journal, 33*(2), 455-488.

THE TIP (3.5)

Assign homework and other projects requiring students to write about connections between mathematics and other subjects.

What the Research Says

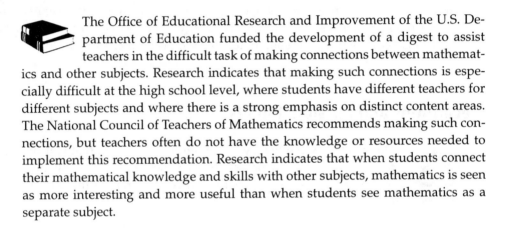

The Office of Educational Research and Improvement of the U.S. Department of Education funded the development of a digest to assist teachers in the difficult task of making connections between mathematics and other subjects. Research indicates that making such connections is especially difficult at the high school level, where students have different teachers for different subjects and where there is a strong emphasis on distinct content areas. The National Council of Teachers of Mathematics recommends making such connections, but teachers often do not have the knowledge or resources needed to implement this recommendation. Research indicates that when students connect their mathematical knowledge and skills with other subjects, mathematics is seen as more interesting and more useful than when students see mathematics as a separate subject.

Classroom Applications

Teachers often feel that they do not have enough time in class to help students connect what they are learning about mathematics with other subject areas, especially when they want students to read and write about these connections. Homework, and other out-of-class assignments, such as reading newspapers and magazines can be excellent ways of addressing this limitation. A resourceful teacher will be able to show students how almost every page of a newspaper contains applications of mathematics. Naturally, the sports pages and the business section are obvious illustrations of mathematics at work in subjects of gymnastics and history or social studies. These connections, although well known to most students, are not always obvious. For example, the "batting average" is actually not an average in the way students understand the term; rather, it is percent or decimal. The most exciting discoveries of mathematics in use in the newspaper are those where the mathematics is embedded in the article, not necessarily those illustrations that give some quantifiers and the like. Asking students to regularly search for good newspaper applications of mathematics and the review of this material in class are excellent ways of connecting mathematics across the curriculum. Students can also research and write about the relationships between mathematics and related topics in other subjects such as elections, taxes, and the stock market in a class in history or social studies; mixtures of solutions and soil composition in a science class; fractals in an art class; as well as scales, chord structures, and chord progressions in a music class.

Precautions and Possible Pitfalls

 One should be careful of using as connectors to other fields, the trivial, or simple, illustrations of numbers being used to quantify a situation. Students may like to use these as their examples; but, because they offer relatively little to connect mathematics to other fields, it would be wise to caution the class not to use these as their examples.

SOURCES

McIntosh, M. (1991). No time for writing in your class? *Mathematics Teacher, 84*(6), 423-433.

Reed, M. K. (1995). *Making mathematical connections in high school.* Columbus, OH: ERIC Clearinghouse for Science, Mathematics, and Environmental Education. (ERIC Document Reproduction Service No. ED 380 310 95)

Vatter, T. (1994). Civic mathematics: A real-life general mathematics course. *Mathematics Teacher, 87*(6), 396-401.

Wood, K. D. (1992). Fostering collaborative reading and writing experiences in mathematics. *Journal of Reading, 36*(2), 96-102.

THE TIP (3.6)

 Find out about your students' families and how their values and practices might affect the students' attitudes and their performance in mathematics.

What the Research Says

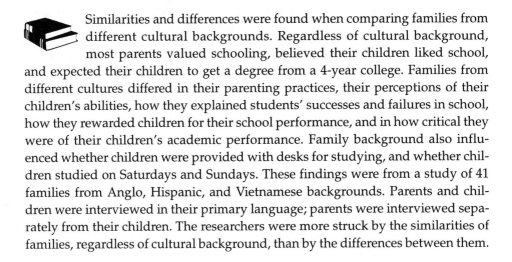 Similarities and differences were found when comparing families from different cultural backgrounds. Regardless of cultural background, most parents valued schooling, believed their children liked school, and expected their children to get a degree from a 4-year college. Families from different cultures differed in their parenting practices, their perceptions of their children's abilities, how they explained students' successes and failures in school, how they rewarded children for their school performance, and in how critical they were of their children's academic performance. Family background also influenced whether children were provided with desks for studying, and whether children studied on Saturdays and Sundays. These findings were from a study of 41 families from Anglo, Hispanic, and Vietnamese backgrounds. Parents and children were interviewed in their primary language; parents were interviewed separately from their children. The researchers were more struck by the similarities of families, regardless of cultural background, than by the differences between them.

Classroom Applications

There are clearly cultural differences with regard to the emphasis on topics and skills taught in school mathematics. Whether these cultural differences are related to youngsters by their parents is something the teacher would be wise to discover through interviews with individual students and in teacher-parent conferences. There may be an unduly high priority in arithmetic skills stressed in one home, whereas in another home, this skill may be somewhat neglected in favor of an understanding of concepts such as proportional thinking. This latter concept is far more prominent in the school curriculum of central European schools than it is in the United States. Furthermore, the time available for study can influence the achievement of a youngster. If the teacher finds out that the children have more time available for homework on the weekend, they may use this opportunity to assign more work to be done then, in addition to maintaining regular homework assignments during the week. If this is not the case, because of religious reasons, for example, the student must pay the price for this misjudgment. In short, teachers should communicate with the home, via the students and the parents, so that the classroom support at home is used properly.

Precautions and Possible Pitfalls

Be careful not to take at "face value" comments made by students about their home life interfering with the school's homework assignments. Students, who see the teacher as very sensitive to being obtrusive to the student's home life, may intentionally try to block progress with "harmless untruths." Precaution is appropriate here!

SOURCE

Lindholm, K. J., & Miura, I. T. (1991, August). *Family influences on mathematics achievement: Anglo, Hispanic, and Vietnamese students.* Paper presented at the annual meeting of the American Psychological Association, San Francisco, CA.

THE TIP (3.7)

☑ Reach out to parents to form a partnership in educating elementary and high school students.

What the Research Says

 Students want their parents to be involved in their education. A high level of parental involvement in children's education generally leads to a high level of academic achievement. Parents frequently are involved with their children's education while children are in elementary school, but often stop being involved once children are in high school. One study looked at 748 urban elementary and secondary school students' (Grade 5, $n = 257$; Grade 7, $n = 257$; Grade 9, $n = 144$; and Grade 11, $n = 90$) requests for and attitudes about their families' involvement in their education. Of these students, 449 were black, 129 were Hispanic, and 121 were white. The study compared high- and low-achieving students in mathematics and English (reading for elementary school students). It also examined whether there were ethnic differences in students' feelings about family involvement. Students in all grades requested parental assistance with schoolwork and had positive attitudes about using their parents as educational resources, although elementary students made more requests and had more positive attitudes than secondary school students. Both high- and low-achieving students showed interest in parental involvement. At the elementary-school level, however, high-achieving Hispanic students in mathematics had more favorable attitudes than did low-achieving Hispanic students in mathematics. Black and Hispanic students were generally more interested in parental involvement than were white students.

Classroom Applications

Teachers should reach out to parents to enhance their involvement and to help them engage in a partnership in their children's education. Many parents are unaware that they have the ability to have an impact on their children's education—even if they are not well educated themselves. Teachers can explain and illustrate for parents how a parent can function as an educational manager, teacher, or both. Some examples of the parent as manager include the following:

- Provide a time, a quiet place, and adequate light for studying. Help the child determine the best time and place to work
- Each night, ask if there is a homework assignment and ask to see it when it has been completed
- Each night, ask about what happened in school
- Have a dictionary accessible and encourage the child to use it
- Find out when tests are to be given, make sure the child has a good night's sleep, and eats breakfast the day of the test
- Visit the school to discuss the child's progress and to find out what can be done at home
- Communicate positive attitudes and expectations about the child's school performance
- Avoid letting a child's household responsibilities assume more importance than schoolwork
- Ask the teacher to prepare a handout explaining to parents what they can do at home to support this partnership

The above can be further reinforced by sending home a regular "newsletter" reminding parents of a role they can play to be supportive of their children. This newsletter can also inform parents of the class' progress.

Precautions and Possible Pitfalls

 If parents do not speak English well, they may be reluctant to communicate with teachers. In such cases, if the teacher cannot speak the parent's language, a community volunteer might act as a school advocate and resource or someone from the school might be able to translate a letter or handout for parents into the parents' native language.

SOURCES

Hartman-Haas, H. J. (1983, April). *Family educational interaction: Focus on the child.* Paper presented at the annual meeting of the American Educational Research Association, Montreal, Canada.

Hartman-Haas, H. J. (1984). Family involvement tips for teachers. *Division of Research Evaluation and Testing Research Bulletin, 3*(1), 1-12.

THE TIP (3.8)

 Inform parents that they should not let media reports about studies of other children change their views of their own children's abilities to be successful in mathematics.

What the Research Says

 Parents may develop misconceptions about their children's abilities as a result of reports in the media. One study examined the impact on parents of a media report on gifted, junior high school students. Extensive media coverage focused on a report of a major gender difference in students' mathematical aptitudes. The study compared parents' views about their children's mathematical aptitudes before and after exposure to the media report. The results showed that the media coverage changed parents' attitudes about their children's mathematical abilities. Fathers of sons and mothers of daughters developed stronger sex-based stereotyped beliefs after the media coverage.

Classroom Applications

For most people, mathematics is a source of frustration. A general reaction to the field by the average parent is to say that they did poorly in the subject themselves, so they tend to accept this from their children. It appears to be a sort of "badge of honor" to admit weakness in mathematics (unlike almost any other subject!). Teachers would be wise to offer periodic workshops for parents—keeping them informed of what is being taught, how it is being presented, and what can be expected of their children, both in performance and results. This sort of workshop experience will also give teachers an opportunity to communicate with parents regularly and to inform them of their individual child's progress and ability to be successful in mathematics. Parents will then be more prepared to interpret reports from the media and other sources. They would also be less likely to succumb to overgeneralizations and stereotypes, which could undermine their child's performance in mathematics.

Precautions and Possible Pitfalls

⚠ Extreme patience must be used when working with parents. Recognize that many of them may have been away from a school setting and the concomitant behavior for many years. Be cautious when reporting frequently on a student's progress, leaving room for improvement and never "close the door" on an individual student, no matter how frustrating the child's progress may be. Remember that some parents have a tendency to overreact to the teacher's comments and that may have deleterious effects.

SOURCE

Jacobs, J. E., & Eccles, J. S. (1985). Gender differences in ability: The impact of media reports on parents. *Educational Researcher, 14*(3), 20-25.

THE TIP (3.9)

 Teachers are knowledge generators. Everyone can benefit when teachers collaborate with researchers from a local college or university to improve learning and instruction in mathematics.

What the Research Says

Teachers and researchers work best together to improve the practice of teaching and learning mathematics when they synthesize their professional knowledge through sustained collaboration. It is most important for teachers to be recognized as knowledge generators and not just translators of knowledge generated by researchers. There must be shared leadership in teacher-researcher collaborations. Research was based on a 54-month study of a collaboration called the Thinking Mathematics Project, which involved the American Federation of Teachers (AFT) and the Learning, Research, and Development Center (LRDC) of the University of Pittsburgh. Expert teachers and cognitive researchers pooled their knowledge about what works best for teaching and learning mathematics. One dimension of the study focused on interactions between the two organizations and documented activities of collaboration building by AFT and LRDC leaders including deciding on and revising priorities, identifying and addressing issues, and identifying factors that affected the value and soundness of the collaboration. The other dimension focused on collaborative activities at the institutional level. Data collection involved observations, interviews, debriefings, surveys, analysis of documents, and informal interactions with teachers and researchers. The collaboration resulted in a set of basic principles for teaching mathematics that are being pilot tested.

Classroom Applications

Using the Thinking Mathematics Project as a model is one way to proceed with this tip. Yet, it should be recognized that collaboration with a nearby institution of higher learning can take on its own form, based on mutual interests. It is helpful to know the format and purview of the Thinking Mathematics Project. Its basic principles include the following:

- Build on students' intuitive knowledge
- Establish a strong sense of number through counting and estimation
- Base instruction on situational story problems
- Use manipulatives to represent the problem situation
- Accept and solicit multiple correct solutions and sometimes even multiple correct answers
- Require students to explain and justify their thinking
- Use a variety of teaching strategies
- Balance conceptual and procedural learning
- Use ongoing assessment to guide instruction
- Adjust the time line for introducing new topics

Precautions and Possible Pitfalls

 Successful collaboration between teachers and researchers is unlikely to happen unless there is shared leadership and unless the traditional model of researchers as being the source of knowledge is rejected. Also, it is difficult to maintain collaboration over an extended period of time, even when the collaboration is recognized as being very important for educational reform. Awareness of this possible problem, as well as recognizing that institutional collaboration is often dependent on individual interest, and when interest wanes, or the parties involved leave their positions, the programs usually end, should motivate participants to keep the agenda relevant and to involve as many people as possible.

SOURCES

Bickel, W. E., & Hattrup, R. A. (1995). Teachers and researchers in collaboration: Reflections on the process. *American Educational Research Journal, 32*(1), 35-62.

Gill, A., & Billups, L. (1992). The power of thinking mathematics. *American Educators Journal, 16*(4), 4-11, 48.

THE TIP (3.10)

Learn about van Hiele's theory and deepen your knowledge of geometry to create lessons with higher-level goals and expectations.

What the Research Says

Teachers can help students learn higher-level mathematical content by deepening their own knowledge about geometry and about van Hiele's theory and research on cognition. A study was conducted with 49 middle school teachers who participated in a 4-week research seminar on van Hiele's work on student cognition in geometry and a 4-week course in geometry. Researchers examined teachers' lesson plans before and after the courses. The results showed that teachers changed their teaching in three ways: what they taught, how they taught, and what characteristics they displayed when teaching. Teachers shifted to higher-level goals and expectations at the next higher level in van Hiele's theory as a result of the courses. According to the teachers, these changes were a direct result of what they had learned about van Hiele's theory and geometry.

Classroom Applications

Real Maths/Maths for All, a curriculum for students aged 12-16, is based on the theory of van Hiele, an internationally known Dutch mathematics teacher and researcher. van Hiele's level theory identifies three levels:

Zero or perceptive level: Students look at the whole problem without analyzing the parts.

First or descriptive level: Students describe the parts and their characteristics, have an intuitive understanding, but there is no reflection on fundamental ideas.

Second or theoretical level: Students' intuitive concepts are formulated more explicitly and students reflect on concepts and on the relationships between problem parts and the whole.

van Hiele recommends a 5-stage teaching-learning process:

Information: Students get materials (e.g., objects, graphs, papers, and so on) to use in exercises.

Structured orientation: Students are assigned specific tasks. Each task is designed to teach students one characteristic of the material they are using.

Expliciting: Students describe the characteristic verbally.

Free orientation: Students are given general tasks that require them to find their own way in a network of relations.

Integration: Students reflect on different solutions, explore relationships between them, and formulate laws of a new and higher-level structure.

Real-life settings are essential features of all mathematics problems in this approach. The lesson design model for this curriculum consists of three stages:

1. *Introduction:* Working with the whole class, the teacher introduces the problem, explores various aspects of it, may give hints about the solution, and places it in an everyday life context.

2. *Group work:* Students work in groups as the teacher observes and manages their cooperative problem solving. When necessary, the teacher deals with individual problems.

3. *Reflection and evaluation:* Students discuss several topics related to their group process and results. The discussion involves identifying all the different solutions and strategies that the groups used to solve the problem, teacher-questioning to explore other possible solution strategies, reformulating and summarizing solutions, and generalizing about solutions.

Sample lessons involve using newspaper ads, deciding which video shop to join as a member, and selling badges as a small business enterprise. The Real Maths curriculum has accompanying teachers' manuals as resources for using real-life situations for mathematical problems and for teaching with heterogeneous, small groups. It also has student materials and videotapes.

Precautions and Possible Pitfalls

Any new approach in the teaching process by a teacher must be done with a modicum of caution. Just as there is no "one size fits all," there is no universally best way to teach. Such decisions must be individually decided based on the unique set of factors that prevail at the time.

SOURCES

Swafford, J. O., Jones, G. A., & Thornton, C. A. (1997). Increased knowledge in geometry and instructional practice. *Journal for Research in Mathematics Education, 28*(4), 467–483.

Terwel, J. (1990). Real Maths in cooperative groups in secondary education. In N. Davidson (Ed.), *Cooperative learning in mathematics* (pp. 228–264). Tucson, AZ: Zephyr.

van Hiele, P. M. (1986). *Structure and insight: A theory of mathematics education.* Orlando, FL: Academic Press.

CHAPTER FOUR

Developing Positive Attitudes About Mathematics

THE TIP (4.1)

 Teach students, especially girls, to believe that success in mathematics results from their strategies and efforts.

What the Research Says

 Recent research shows that one of the major factors influencing students' motivation is how they explain their successes and failures. There are four explanations that students commonly give for their academic successes and failures: ability, effort, task difficulty, and luck. In one study, 279 junior high school students completed a questionnaire on their beliefs about mathematics achievement. The questionnaire was completed both before and after a mathematics exam. The results showed that girls tend to attribute failure in mathematics to low ability and bad luck and they tend to attribute success in mathematics to high ability. Also, girls were more likely than boys to hide their papers after failure and to have less pride in their successes. These results led to the conclusion that how students explain their successes and failures in mathematics depends on students' gender. Teachers should help students in general, and girls in particular, to realize that they have the ability to control their own academic destiny, and that the specific strategies and types of efforts they make, or don't make, lead to specific outcomes.

Classroom Applications

Teachers can teach students how to convert failures into future successes by doing an "error analysis" using the following model:

What was the incorrect answer? What is the correct answer?

Why did you have the wrong answer? Be specific.

How can you prevent that same type of mistake in the future? What did you learn that you need to remember for future success?

Have students compare an example of their successful performance with an example of their unsuccessful performance so they can determine how the situations differed. Help students identify patterns in their successes and failures so they can repeat the use of successful strategies with confidence, and overcome failures with more effort and better strategies. Teachers can generate some positive feelings in the learner by presenting some simple exercises, ones in which success is reasonably expected. Hopefully, if presented cleverly, these simple exercises will generate a positive attitude that will carry over to somewhat more complicated problems or exercises on the same topic.

Precautions and Pitfalls

Sometimes students show a pattern of "learned helplessness" and feel they have no control over their own destiny. These students usually feel that other powerful people, such as the teacher, and luck or fate determine what happens to them. These students tend to externalize responsibility for and control over their academic performance. They may also feel that they do not have the ability to succeed. Such students need special guidance in learning how specific thinking, learning, and problem-solving strategies lead to specific academic outcomes. When giving exercises designed to boost positive attitudes, make sure they are not too simple. If success comes too easily it will not have much significance or impact.

SOURCE

Stipek, D. J., & Gralinski, J. H. (1991). Gender differences in children's achievement-related beliefs and emotional responses to success and failure in mathematics. *Journal of Educational Psychology, 83*(3), 361-371.

THE TIP (4.2)

 When trying to determine how to motivate students' interest in mathematics, teachers should differentiate between personal and situational interest and use both forms to increase students' motivation to learn mathematics. Teachers also need to be able to both stimulate and maintain students' interest.

What the Research Says

 Teachers can draw on the different types of interest that students have in mathematics. Personal interest is what students bring with them to the classroom or other environment; situational interest is something that is acquired by participating in an activity in the classroom or another situation. Whereas personal interest emphasizes the importance of working with individual differences in motivation, situational interest emphasizes the importance of the teacher creating an appropriate setting to develop the students' interest in mathematics. Teachers should also differentiate between factors that stimulate student interest and those that maintain student interest. Computers, puzzles, and group work tend to stimulate interest in mathematics while meaningfulness and involvement tend to maintain student interest.

In a study of 350 high school students from three high schools, students were administered an interest survey with seven scales: personal interest, situational interest, meaningfulness, involvement, puzzles, computers, and group work. Students rated items on a 6-point scale ranging from *strongly disagree* to *strongly agree*. Most students were white and were in 13 college preparatory algebra or geometry classes. The results showed that situational interest in secondary school mathematics classrooms is complex, having five different components: meaningfulness, puzzles, computers, group work, and involvement. Increasing student involvement in mathematics appears to be especially beneficial for enhancing situational interest.

Classroom Applications

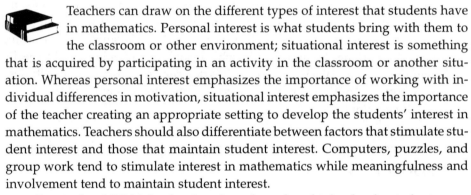 There are many techniques for creating situational motivation in the classroom. Sometimes the motivation lies in the material and other times it is dependent on the manner in which the activity is presented. Here are ten techniques for motivating a lesson:

- Indicate a void in the students' knowledge (through self-realization)
- Present a challenge

- Show sequential achievement
- Indicate the usefulness of a topic (real world application)
- Use recreational mathematics
- Tell a pertinent story
- Consider a current events story that can relate to the topic of the day
- Get students actively involved in justifying mathematical curiosities
- Use teacher-made or commercially prepared materials or devices
- Relate a topic to be "motivated" to another area of the students' studies

For example, when motivating a topic (or lesson) on digit problems in the algebra class, or when the class is beginning to understand the workings of the decimal system (algebraically), you might have students try to explain the following mathematical novelty:

Why does the following arithmetic always result in the same number, 1,089?

Do the following:

> Choose any 3-digit number (where the units and hundreds digit are not the same).
> Subtract the number with the digits reversed.
> To this difference, add the numbers with the digits reversed.
> Your result should be 1,089. Why?

Remember, when possible try to direct motivational devices to girls!

Precautions and Possible Pitfalls

 The primary precaution when doing a motivational activity is to make sure that it is appropriate for the intended students in both interest and level. In addition, ensure that it leads to the topic being motivated rather than distracting from it. If successful, try to modify other lessons to maximize student interest so that the usual classwork does not become a bore compared with this highly interesting activity.

SOURCE

Mitchell, M. (1993). Situational interest: Its multifaceted structure in the secondary school mathematics classroom. *Journal of Educational Psychology, 85*(3), 424-436.

THE TIP (4.3)

 Use different motivational strategies for girls and boys.

What the Research Says

When it comes to motivation, girls tend to be generalists; boys tend to be specialists. Interest, rather than intellect, often lies at the heart of the differences between boys and girls in mathematics. Girls tend to be interested in a wide range of subjects, whereas boys tend to concentrate their interests more narrowly. A study was conducted with 457 students; 338 students attended special mathematics- and science-oriented schools while 119 students attended regular schools but had excellent grades in mathematics, physics, and chemistry. At the beginning of a 2-year study, students were asked to rate their interest in later studying mathematics. Almost twice the percentage of girls showed interest in studying mathematics later as did the boys. Several times over a period of 2 years, teachers were asked to rank their students' abilities in mathematics. The ranking of the girls became worse over time.

Girls and boys were asked to rate how much they liked doing a variety of mathematical/physical and linguistic/literary tasks. Mathematical/physical tasks included finding variations of solutions to problems, solving especially difficult tasks, creating tasks by oneself, doing puzzles, and playing chess. Linguistic/literary tasks included making puns; following dialogues in literature, drama, or a radio play; having discussions with intellectuals; and finding contradictions or inconsistencies in texts. The results showed that girls are interested in a variety of areas and that they tended to concentrate their studying in all subjects rather than investing in one at the expense of the others, as the boys tended to do. Over time, girls' interests expanded while boys' interests narrowed.

Classroom Applications

On average, girls often seem not to be as good in mathematics as boys. This phenomenon does not happen because girls have less talent in mathematics than boys. It is because of their greater interest in a wide range of topics. Consequently, girls will be more easily motivated if mathematical facts touch a wider range of subjects.

For example:

1. Relate the quadratic equation in general to that of the golden section, which can be shown as it exists in art or architecture;

2. Relate perspectivity in geometry to paintings, etchings, and drawings;

3. Connect mathematical structures with Bach's music;

4. Relate famous mathematicians like Pythagoras and Euclid to philosophy, history, or both. You might have students work on projects that correspond with their interests and write papers or reports.

Precautions and Possible Pitfalls

 Don't be disappointed if your efforts to motivate girls do not produce the desired effects. Continue to give girls the opportunity to demonstrate their abilities to achieve in mathematics.

SOURCE

Pollmer, K. (1991). Was behindert hochbegabte Mädchen, Erfolg im Mathematikunterricht zu erreichen? [What handicaps highly gifted girls from being successful in mathematics?]. *Psychologie in Erziehung und Unterricht, 38,* 28-36.

THE TIP (4.4)

 Find out about your students' motivation regarding mathematics and use that knowledge to refine your instruction.

What the Research Says

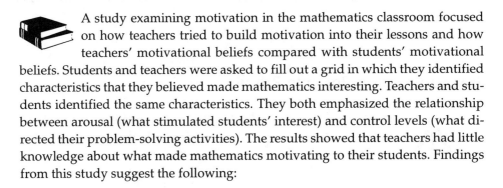 A study examining motivation in the mathematics classroom focused on how teachers tried to build motivation into their lessons and how teachers' motivational beliefs compared with students' motivational beliefs. Students and teachers were asked to fill out a grid in which they identified characteristics that they believed made mathematics interesting. Teachers and students identified the same characteristics. They both emphasized the relationship between arousal (what stimulated students' interest) and control levels (what directed their problem-solving activities). The results showed that teachers had little knowledge about what made mathematics motivating to their students. Findings from this study suggest the following:

Teachers need to learn about what makes mathematics interesting to students.

Teachers need to pay attention to individual differences in student motivation.

When teachers know about their students' motivational beliefs, they are more capable of refining their instruction so that students are interested in mathematics.

Classroom Applications

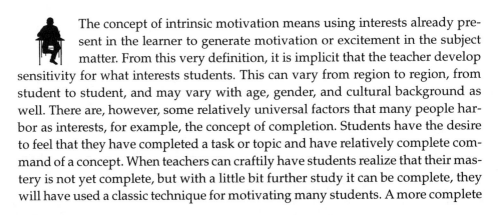 The concept of intrinsic motivation means using interests already present in the learner to generate motivation or excitement in the subject matter. From this very definition, it is implicit that the teacher develop sensitivity for what interests students. This can vary from region to region, from student to student, and may vary with age, gender, and cultural background as well. There are, however, some relatively universal factors that many people harbor as interests, for example, the concept of completion. Students have the desire to feel that they have completed a task or topic and have relatively complete command of a concept. When teachers can craftily have students realize that their mastery is not yet complete, but with a little bit further study it can be complete, they will have used a classic technique for motivating many students. A more complete

treatment of this motivational technique can be found in *Teaching Secondary School Mathematics: Techniques and Enrichment Units* by A. S. Posamentier and J. Stepelman (1998).

Precautions and Possible Pitfalls

Teachers need to cultivate the ability to determine what really motivates their specific students instead of assuming students are motivated by the same things that motivate the teachers themselves. To motivate students effectively, problems and topics must be appropriate in their content, structure, and level of difficulty.

SOURCES

Middleton, J. A. (1995). A study of intrinsic motivation in the mathematics classroom: A personal constructs approach. *Journal of Research in Mathematics Education, 26*(3), 254-279.

Schiefele, A., & Csikszentonikalyi, Z. (1995). Motivation and ability as factors in mathematics experience and achievement. *Journal of Research in Mathematics Education, 26*(2), 163-181.

THE TIP (4.5)

 If you have students who are not highly motivated to learn mathematics, incorporate motivational skills training into your mathematics instruction.

What the Research Says

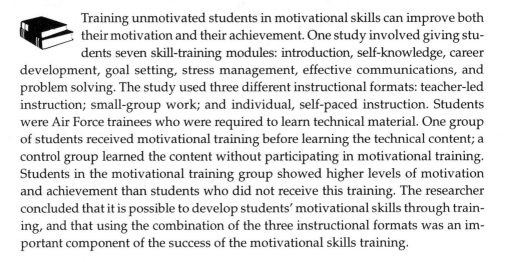 Training unmotivated students in motivational skills can improve both their motivation and their achievement. One study involved giving students seven skill-training modules: introduction, self-knowledge, career development, goal setting, stress management, effective communications, and problem solving. The study used three different instructional formats: teacher-led instruction; small-group work; and individual, self-paced instruction. Students were Air Force trainees who were required to learn technical material. One group of students received motivational training before learning the technical content; a control group learned the content without participating in motivational training. Students in the motivational training group showed higher levels of motivation and achievement than students who did not receive this training. The researcher concluded that it is possible to develop students' motivational skills through training, and that using the combination of the three instructional formats was an important component of the success of the motivational skills training.

Classroom Applications

 A variety of techniques can be used for motivational skills training. Some are described in reference to the seven modules used in the research described previously.

1. *Introduction:* Explain the purpose of motivational skills training. Introduce students to the concepts of personal responsibility and positive self-control, and how these attitudes engender feelings of competence. Introduce students to strategies for controlling negative attitudes, strategies such as monitoring self-messages and focusing on positive self-talk.

2. *Self-knowledge:* Help students examine conflicts in their own values and beliefs and give them strategies for resolving such conflicts. Explain the role of values and beliefs in helping them define themselves and establish priorities based on what is most important to them.

3. Career development: Use students' self-knowledge to examine career options, to develop decision-making skills, and to make career goals and plans.

4. *Goal setting:* Describe the purpose of goals as motivating and directing behavior, explain the difference between short- and long-term goals, teach them how to systematically think about and set personal goals, and give them exercises that require them to set specific short- and long-term goals.

5. *Stress management:* Explain and demonstrate a variety of stress reduction techniques, such as deep breathing, creative visualization, positive self-talk, and progressive muscle relaxation. Explain how negative self-talk, misconceptions about learning, and erroneous perceptions can produce stress. Explain the importance of reducing anxiety before it gets out of control and interferes with learning, test performance, or both.

6. *Effective communications:* Explain the importance of effective speaking, listening, and giving feedback so that others understand their wants, needs, feelings, and concerns. Teach students listening strategies such as "paraphrasing," "reflecting the feeling," and showing empathy. Teach them to think about how they are speaking (e.g., tone, pace, volume) in addition to what they are speaking about. Teach them to be aware of their own and others' nonverbal communications. Finally, teach them to be sensitive to cultural differences in communication.

7. *Problem solving:* Show students how they have been using problem-solving approaches throughout the motivational skills training and in other areas of their lives. Explain and demonstrate a model for effective problem solving, and give students practice applying the model to a variety of problems. (See *Problem-Solving Strategies for Efficient and Elegant Solutions: A Resource for the Mathematics Teacher,* by A. S. Posamentier and S. Krulik [1998].)

Precautions and Possible Pitfalls

Use a combination of these three formats for motivational skills training: (a) some material is presented by a teacher, (b) some work is done in small groups, and (c) some work should involve students working alone, self-pacing their instruction. Teachers should make motivational material more personally relevant and meaningful to students by describing some of their own experiences, showing genuine personal interest in the students, being a positive role model, and by conveying how the motivational skills will help students in their future endeavors.

SOURCE

McCombs, B. (1984). Processes and skills underlying continuing intrinsic motivation to learn: Toward a definition of motivational skills training interventions. *Educational Psychologist, 19*(4), 199-218.

THE TIP (4.6)

 Playing makes mathematics easier and more fun.

What the Research Says

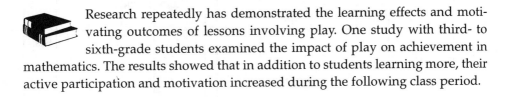 Research repeatedly has demonstrated the learning effects and motivating outcomes of lessons involving play. One study with third- to sixth-grade students examined the impact of play on achievement in mathematics. The results showed that in addition to students learning more, their active participation and motivation increased during the following class period.

Classroom Applications

 The activity described next, which is like a game show, was used in the experiment described in the previous section. You may adapt it for your students and mathematical content.

1. Preparation for the quiz
   - Create a transparency with a basic diagram with 36 squares (see Figure 4.1)
   - Six questions for luck and six questions for risk are distributed at random on a hidden copy of the basic diagram (see Figure 4.2)

   Make sure you have enough of the luck- and risk-type questions. Students like them and they motivate students to play.

Figure 4.1. The Big Prize

	1	2	3	4	5	6
A						
B						
C						
D						
E						
F						

Figure 4.2. The Big Prize

	1	2	3	4	5	6
A		Luck			Risk	
B				Risk		Luck
C			Risk	Luck		
D	Luck	Luck				
E			Luck		Risk	
F	Luck					Risk

2. Preliminary round

   - Every student has to answer three questions
   - The student is allowed to personally select the mathematical topic (e.g., oral multiplication)
   - Every correct answer earns two points for the student
   - Six points is the maximum per student

3. Main round

   - Every student starts the main round with the number of points he or she has accumulated in the preliminary round
   - As soon as the moderator asks a question, students can raise their hands to answer
   - The student who raises his or her hand first is allowed to answer the question
   - The student who earned the last points has to select the square for the next student
   - Each luck-square gives five points for the correct answer
   - Each risk-square allows the student to as much as double the number of points that have been accumulated. The student decides how many points of his or her score he or she wants to risk. If the student correctly answers the question, the

points he or she has risked will be added. If the student gives an incorrect answer, the number of risked points will be subtracted from his or her score

- The remaining squares provide 1 point added for each correct answer and 1 point subtracted for each wrong answer

4. Course of the quiz (this can be given out to students)

- Class and teacher elect people for the following roles:
  - Moderator (this could be the teacher)
  - Assistant (who covers the answered squares)
  - Three counters (scorekeepers)
  - Referee (decides about the order of students, who raised their hands first, and so on)
  - Six game players
- Arrange the chairs in a horseshoe. Players can sit at the front and the "audience" can sit along the sides
- The counters announce the score at the end of the preliminary round
- The player who has the highest score starts the main round. In case of tied score between several students, the winner will be decided by the results of a play-off question
- The transparency with the basic diagram (Figure 4.1) is displayed on an overhead projector. The moderator keeps the transparency that appears in Figure 4.2
- The player who starts the main round chooses one square (e.g., square D4)
- The assistant now covers this square with a stone or the like
- The moderator asks the question
- According to the order in which hands were raised, students give their answers until the correct answer is given. The referee observes the correct order and makes sure that no one is called on out of turn
- If a square with *Luck* or *Risk* is selected, only the student who has chosen it is allowed to answer the question. Only if he or she gives a wrong answer does the question becomes open for the other players
- The quiz is finished when all squares are gone
- The student with the highest score wins

Besides just using written tests, a teacher should look for fun and efficient ways to check knowledge, abilities, and skills.

Precautions and Possible Pitfalls

Playing games during lessons requires constant and strict organization. Otherwise, you will produce more problems than motivation. Give very precise directions for playing the game and for how you expect students to behave. In case students start to misbehave, stop the game and try it again during one of the next lessons.

SOURCE

Borst, O. (1994). Der große Preis. Ein Spiel für alle Klassenstufen und Lerninhalte [The big prize. A quiz for all grades and all subject matter]. *Mathematica Didactica, 17*(1), 106-118.

THE TIP (4.7)

Increase your understanding of the factors that affect students' attitudes before and after testing. You may be surprised!

What the Research Says

Students fear tests less than usually is assumed. The widespread negative attitude of many students before a test is mainly due to their competence in the content they are being tested on rather than the fact that they are being tested. Research has shown that the student's attitudes did not deteriorate, as was predicted, when the student took a test. A study was conducted to investigate specific emotional states of students in different school situations. Four attitudinal dimensions were examined: negative attitude (depression, anxiety, boredom, tiredness, nervousness), positive attitude (good mood, activity, carelessness, relaxation), eagerness to learn (concentration, sympathy), and aggressive excitement (aggressiveness, annoyance). Participants included 126 students; 72 boys and 54 girls. The average age was 11.5 years. Students judged 58 items using a 6-point scale. The items asked about their emotions before and after a test and about lessons with and without testing. The researchers hypothesized that (a) all four dimensions would show differences before and after a test; (b) students would show different attitudes with and without a test; (c) girls and boys would show different attitudes; and (d) students' attitudes would depend on their grades.

The results showed that (a) only two of the four dimensions showed differences before and after the test—they were positive attitude and eagerness to learn; (b) in general, both girls and boys had better attitudes after a lesson; (c) girls showed less eagerness to learn than boys; (d) taking the test did not produce the expected deterioration of students' emotional state; (e) girls' emotions did not differ before and after lessons or with and without tests—in both cases girls had more negative attitudes than boys; and (f) students who got good grades showed better attitudes before the tests than students who did not get good grades.

Classroom Applications

Teachers tend to notice a difference in the attitudes of girls and boys toward testing; girls, in general, have a less positive attitude toward testing than boys. The research suggests that students' attitudes depend on their capability more than their anxiety about a test. A negative attitude of a student before as well as after a test can signal to the teacher that it is necessary to support test results with careful comments (see Tip 2.13 in Chapter 2 about students' perception of marks). If you provide students with feedback that they can use to improve their performance in the area being tested, and they start getting better grades because they have learned from their mistakes, you can expect students to show more positive attitudes, regardless of testing. If you notice that students who usually have positive attitudes have changed and suddenly have negative attitudes, this observation can be a sign that students are having difficulty learning the content you are teaching.

Precautions and Possible Pitfalls

Do not consider every significant change in a student's attitude as an expression of a learning problem. There are many personal factors that can cause changes in students' emotional states.

SOURCE

Chemnitz, G. (1979). Emotionale Reaktion von Schülern während einer Schulstunde mit und ohne Klassenarbeit [Emotional reactions of pupils during school lessons with and without tests]. *Psychologie in Erziehung und Unterricht, 26,* 170-173.

THE TIP (4.8)

 Find out what makes students rate a mathematical task as difficult so that you can increase the difficulty of exercises and tests more effectively.

What the Research Says

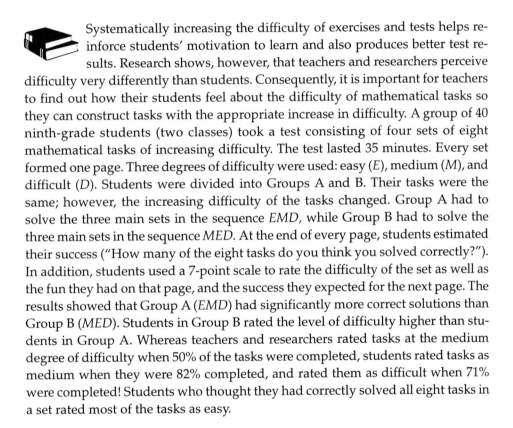 Systematically increasing the difficulty of exercises and tests helps reinforce students' motivation to learn and also produces better test results. Research shows, however, that teachers and researchers perceive difficulty very differently than students. Consequently, it is important for teachers to find out how their students feel about the difficulty of mathematical tasks so they can construct tasks with the appropriate increase in difficulty. A group of 40 ninth-grade students (two classes) took a test consisting of four sets of eight mathematical tasks of increasing difficulty. The test lasted 35 minutes. Every set formed one page. Three degrees of difficulty were used: easy (*E*), medium (*M*), and difficult (*D*). Students were divided into Groups A and B. Their tasks were the same; however, the increasing difficulty of the tasks changed. Group A had to solve the three main sets in the sequence *EMD*, while Group B had to solve the three main sets in the sequence *MED*. At the end of every page, students estimated their success ("How many of the eight tasks do you think you solved correctly?"). In addition, students used a 7-point scale to rate the difficulty of the set as well as the fun they had on that page, and the success they expected for the next page. The results showed that Group A (*EMD*) had significantly more correct solutions than Group B (*MED*). Students in Group B rated the level of difficulty higher than students in Group A. Whereas teachers and researchers rated tasks at the medium degree of difficulty when 50% of the tasks were completed, students rated tasks as medium when they were 82% completed, and rated them as difficult when 71% were completed! Students who thought they had correctly solved all eight tasks in a set rated most of the tasks as easy.

Classroom Applications

 If teachers choose to increase the degree of difficulty, they need information about students' feelings. To get this information, teachers can create a test and link it with questions that have students rate the difficulty of each item on a 7-point scale such as the one presented next.

Figure 4.3

1	2	3	4	5	6	7
Very easy	Pretty easy	Easy	Medium difficulty	Difficult	Pretty difficult	Very difficult

Similarly, teachers can investigate students' enjoyment and their expectations. Sometimes it is wise not to make assumptions about how students feel, or trust your own theories or "sixth sense" about students' reactions. Instead, teachers should ask the students themselves. One way to do this is by interviewing students. Another way is to administer a questionnaire and obtain statistical data on students' feelings about tasks. This provides objective information that can help the teacher design tasks consistent with students' abilities as well as their motivation. In addition, students might enjoy having their feelings about academic tasks examined.

Precautions and Possible Pitfalls

 Do not ask students about their feelings about task difficulty and enjoyment too often. Otherwise, you are likely to get a distorted impression of the students' estimation of an assignment's difficulty and students may deceive their teacher to make exercises and/or tests easier!

SOURCE

Kloep, M., & Weimann, F. (1982). Aufgabenschwierigkeit und Mathematikleistungen bei Realschülern. Zum Problem der mittleren Aufgabenschwierigkeit [Homework difficulty and mathematics achievement of high school students as related to homework problems of medium difficulty]. *Psychologie in Erziehung und Unterricht, 29*, 76-80.

THE TIP (4.9)

 To reduce math anxiety, focus on both the thoughts and emotions of the students.

What the Research Says

There are two different components of math anxiety, cognitive (intellectual) and affective (emotional), which are similar in boys and girls and in younger and older children. One study examined math anxiety in 6th- to 12th-grade children ($N = 564$; 298 boys, 266 girls) as part of a comprehensive, longitudinal study of children's attitudes, values, and beliefs about mathematics. Students were administered two questionnaires: The Student Attitude Questionnaire and the Math Anxiety Questionnaire. The Math Anxiety Questionnaire has 19 items and examines six types of anxious student reactions to mathematics: dislike, worry, fear, dread, confusion/frustration, and lack of confidence. Students rated items on 7-point scales. Scales responses ranged from *not at all at ease and relaxed* to *very much at ease and relaxed*, and *I never feel this way* to *I very often feel this way*. The results showed that girls and boys, as well as older and younger children, have math anxiety made up of two components. One component is intellectual or cognitive; the other component is emotional or affective. The intellectual component primarily involves worrying about failure and its consequences. The emotional component involves fear, feeling nervous, and being uncomfortable. Students with high levels of math anxiety tend to worry too much about what will happen if they fail. Worrying too much about performance is disruptive. It creates a negative emotional state that interferes with achievement in mathematics.

Results showed that the emotional component of math anxiety had a stronger and more negative relationship to children's perceptions of their ability and their performance, and to their actual math performance, than did the worry component. The worry component had a stronger and more positive relationship to the importance children place on math, and their reported actual effort in math, than did the affective component. Girls reported stronger negative emotional reactions to math than boys did. Ninth graders reported they experienced the most worry about math and sixth graders reported the least amount of worry. There was relatively little change in math anxiety scores from junior through senior high school.

Classroom Applications

 Ask questions of students and listen to how they think about mathematics.

Analyze students' errors and identify recurring patterns. Help students convert failures to improvement plans so they will be more successful in the future.

Pay attention to body language as well as hidden verbal messages that reflect how students feel about mathematics in general, and how they feel about the particular problem they are working on. Show acceptance and don't be judgmental about their feelings. View students as capable of learning even when they doubt it themselves.

Reeducate students about the learning process. Help them understand that learning is a long, slow, gradual process that involves trial and error, confusion, hard work, and failure as part of normal and natural learning. Forgetting things and making mistakes doesn't mean you're stupid.

Use everyday life applications so that mathematics isn't a scary and obscure mystery.

Precautions and Possible Pitfalls

 Students' misconceptions about the learning process may contribute to their anxiety, erode their confidence, and interfere with learning. For example, a student might expect a problem to be solved quickly, and give up when it isn't. A teacher's awareness of this syndrome can be helpful in dismantling it both before it becomes deeply entrenched in the student as well as after it has already become deeply entrenched.

SOURCES

Gourgey, A. (1992). Tutoring developmental mathematics: Overcoming anxiety and fostering independent learning. *Journal of Developmental Education, 15*(3), 10-14.

Wigfield, A., & Meece, J. (1988). Math anxiety in elementary and secondary school students. *Journal of Educational Psychology, 80*(2), 210-216.

THE TIP (4.10)

 Praise mistakes!

What the Research Says

Mistakes are desirable! Most teachers consider mistakes as something forbidden. They immediately correct mistakes in the text, on the blackboard, on posters, in exercise books, and in every student's answer. Prohibiting mistakes produces anxiety about making mistakes and accordingly students become inhibited. This attitude toward mistakes easily can become a heavy burden, especially when there is time pressure. It can also cause students to stop using traditional tools such as a calculator.

In one study, students and teachers ($N = 38$) were asked to solve the following problem within 2 minutes and to write down the answer.

> A customer buys a pocketknife for $6.00. He pays with a $10 bill. Because the owner of the shop does not have enough change, he goes to his neighbor and gets change for the bill. He gives $4.00 in change back to the customer. After the customer left the shop, the neighbor came over and said, "The bill is counterfeit! I want my $10 back!" The shop owner quickly gave back a real $10 bill to his neighbor. How much loss does the shop owner sustain if he bought the pocketknife at a price of $5.00 and if he does not count his loss of income?

Teachers' answers:

Figure 4.4

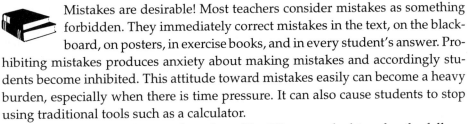

Number of Teachers	5	7	12	9	5
Answer	$10.00	$15.00	$19.00	none	correct

The distribution of teachers' answers is equivalent to the students! Teachers gave the following reasons for making their mistakes: time pressure, feeling controlled, being in public, and lack of concentration.

Classroom Applications

This kind of stress happens to almost every student in almost every lesson. Therefore, a teacher has to be careful when reacting to students' errors that result from stress. This works if the teacher reacts by giving small doses of help, so that the student can partially solve the problem and has some degree of success experience. In addition, you can use mistakes in creative ways, such as blueprints for student self-correction and as wrong-answer choices for a multiple choice test!

Creating anxiety in students about making mistakes depends on the teacher's reaction to mistakes. Teachers generally react on different levels. The first level involves informing the student that a mistake has been made. Subsequent levels usually involve giving substantial or formal help. The teacher's feedback can assume a variety of forms, from insulting to neutral to encouraging.

Examples of insulting the student who made mistakes:

- "Nonsense! Pay better attention!"
- "Sleepyhead! Your answer is rubbish!"
- "If you open your mouth just rubbish comes out!"

Examples for neutral marking of mistakes, without evaluating the student who made them:

- "It is not right!"
- "That's wrong!"
- "There is some mistake!"

Examples of encouraging the student who made a mistake:

- "I am afraid that was not quite correct!"
- "Almost right! Try it again!"
- "Good idea, but, unfortunately not the right direction!"
- "Unfortunately wrong! If you continue thinking about it, you certainly will get the right answer!"

Creative use of mistakes:

Mistakes can be used to uncover wrong ways of thinking. Therefore you should give problems that have several plausible solutions. Suggestions for solutions can be reasoned and discussed. Figure 4.5 shows this schematically. Discussions about how to solve the problem can occur in groups. Problems with several plausible solutions are quite rare. It is also possible to work with mistakes if students know the correct solution. Then they have to analyze their mistake. Figure 4.6 shows this schematically.

Figure 4.5

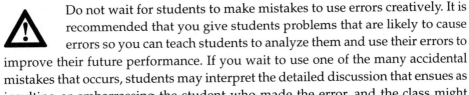

Why is answer 1, 2, or 3 correct?
Why is answer 1, 2, or 3 wrong?

Figure 4.6

Why is answer 1 wrong?
(How the wrong answer is argued? What was the (wrong) way of thinking? What was mixed up?

Precautions and Possible Pitfalls

Do not wait for students to make mistakes to use errors creatively. It is recommended that you give students problems that are likely to cause errors so you can teach students to analyze them and use their errors to improve their future performance. If you wait to use one of the many accidental mistakes that occurs, students may interpret the detailed discussion that ensues as insulting or embarrassing the student who made the error, and the class might rebel against the wonderfully beneficial activity of error analysis!

SOURCE

Morawietz, H. (1997). Fehler kreativ nutzen, Streß verringern, Unterricht öffnen [Creative use of mistakes, reducing stress, and beginning lessons]. *Pädagogik und Schulalltag, 52*(2), 232-245.

THE TIP (4.11)

 Be aware of students' different levels of test anxiety as it relates to different subject areas, and use a variety of techniques to help them overcome their test anxiety.

What the Research Says

Students have different degrees of test anxiety for different subject areas. One study compared 196 first-year college students' self-reports of test anxiety in mathematics, physical sciences, English, and social studies. Students were administered the Worry-Emotionality scale in which they rated their anxiety about tests in one of these four subjects. The directions asked them to imagine they were taking a test in mathematics, for example, and to rate their feelings on a 5-point scale ranging from *I would not feel that way at all* = 1 to *I would feel that way very strongly* = 5. Questions included "I would feel my heart beating fast" and "I would feel that I should have studied more for that test." In rank order from most test anxiety to least test anxiety, the subjects were the following: physical sciences, mathematics, English, and social studies. For elementary and secondary school students, test anxiety is often developed from a combination of factors. These factors include parents' early reactions to their children's poor test performance, students' comparisons of their performance with other students as well as their own prior test performance, and increasingly strict evaluation practices as students progressed through school. For low-achieving students, failure experiences tend to increase test anxiety. For high-achieving students, unrealistically high parental, peer, and self-expectations tend to increase test anxiety. Some classroom practices affect test anxiety. Presenting material in an organized way and making sure it isn't too hard tends to improve the performance of test-anxious students.

Classroom Applications

Test anxiety interferes with test performance. Students waste mental energy on anxiety that they could be using to answer the test questions. There are many strategies teachers can suggest and demonstrate to students to help them relax. First, find out what strategies they already use. Share with them techniques you use to relax. Try to reduce the pressure students feel from being evaluated by tests. Using other assessment strategies, in addition to tests, can help reduce the pressure of being evaluated by tests and the corresponding test anxiety. Help students learn to differentiate between constructive and destructive instances of anxiety. In constructive or facilitative anxiety, students see tests as challenging experiences. In destructive or debilitative anxiety, students see tests as negative self-evaluation experiences. Teach students to become aware of and control their anxiety before, during, and after testing. For example, ask them "What thoughts go through your mind before taking a test?" "What kinds of thoughts do you have while you are taking a test?" Help students improve their study strategies and test-taking skills. Demonstrate and encourage the use of the assorted relaxation techniques described next.

Deep breathing. With erect posture, breathe in deeply through the nose and hold your breath for a count of 8-10. Then, slowly exhale through the mouth, counting 8-10. Repeat this procedure several times until relaxation occurs.

Muscle relaxation. (a) *Tension-relaxation:* Tighten and then relax a muscle or set of muscles, such as your shoulders, that normally store considerable tension. Hold the muscles in a tensed state for a few seconds and then let go. Repeat this sequence with the same muscles a few times and then move on to other muscles. (b) *Self-hypnosis:* Sit straight in a chair with arms and legs uncrossed, feet flat on the floor and palms on top of your thighs. Progressively relax your body, from toes to head, systematically focusing on one part at a time. Concentrate on tuning into your bodily sensations, allowing your muscles to relax, becoming more aware of what it feels like when your muscles are relaxed. Talk to yourself (aloud or silently) telling yourself to loosen up and lessen the tightness. When the body is relaxed, it is more receptive to positive self-talk. Build up your self-confidence at this point. For example, "I know I can do well on this test!"

Creative visualization. Guide students in engaging in success-imagery minutes, days, and weeks before testing. (a) *Olympic success:* Tell them to try what the Olympic athletes do to develop confidence in their performance. Picture yourself in a tense situation, such as taking a test, and visualize yourself looking over the test, seeing the questions, and feeling secure about the answers. Imagine yourself answering the questions without too much difficulty. Complete the picture by imagining yourself turning in the paper and leaving the room assured that you did your best. (b) *Relaxing place:* Where do your students feel most at peace? One spot could be at the ocean. Have students identify a place and use all of their senses to imagine themselves there and how they feel when they are there. Guide them in an activity such as: "Watch" the waves with their white caps rolling up the shoreline onto the beach. "Listen" to the waves and the seagulls. "Smell" the salty air and "feel" your fingers and toes in the warm, soft, and grainy sand.

Precautions and Possible Pitfalls

Whatever a teacher decides to do in this regard must be done with a modicum of reserve, assessing the audience and their reaction. Not all suggestions work with all students. Make sure to encourage students not to give up if the first relaxation technique doesn't work. Often these techniques need to be practiced to be successful, and often students must experiment with a variety of techniques to determine which ones work best for them. Ask your students questions to see whether gender differences, cultural differences, or both might affect the use of these suggestions and to elicit ideas not previously considered by the teacher.

SOURCES

Everson, H. T., Tobias, S., Hartman, H., & Gourgey, A. (1993). Test anxiety and the curriculum: The subject matters. *Anxiety, Stress, and Coping, 6*, 1-8.

Hartman, H. (1997). *Human learning and instruction.* New York: City College of City University of New York.

Wigfield, A., & Eccles, J. S. (1989). Test anxiety in elementary and secondary school students. *Educational Psychologist, 24*(2), 159-183.

THE TIP (4.12)

 Praise, encourage, and help your older students.

What the Research Says

Although older students often seem to avoid teachers' praise, research has shown that even older students care about being praised by the teacher. How do older and younger students compare with each other in how they feel about how their teachers treat them? A study was conducted with 14 teachers, 7 were primary school teachers who had a total of 194 students in Grades 1 to 4; 7 were secondary school teachers, who had 167 students in Grades 5 to 10. Over a period of 8 months, students repeatedly filled out an anonymous 18-item questionnaire on their feelings about how teachers treated them. Questions addressed issues including teacher behaviors of friendliness, praise, encouragement, fairness, favoritism, displays of anger, patience, and receptiveness to students' ideas. For each of the 18 items, students had to choose between whether teachers did or did not treat them in the ways described. For example, "The teacher praises me" or "The teacher doesn't praise me." The results showed that older and younger students had remarkably similar feelings. Older students, however, generally were more critical about their teachers than younger students. The most striking differences between older and younger students were in the following six areas:

  a. The teacher praises me
  b. I like the teacher's ideas
  c. I like taking an active part in the teacher's lessons
  d. The teacher encourages me
  e. The teacher helps me
  f. The teacher listens to what I say

In the first five areas (a-e), a smaller percentage of older students were satisfied with their teachers' behaviors than were the younger students. In the last area (f), a higher percentage of older students were satisfied with their teachers' behaviors than were the younger students.

Classroom Applications

Especially for mathematics lessons, it is said that the communication between teachers and students seems too factual and unemotional. Older students, in particular, would benefit from more teacher praise, help, and encouragement. In mathematics, it is especially important to be sensitive when dealing with students who lack self-confidence in their mathematical abilities. Often teachers do not know how their own behavior severely frustrates students. Sometimes a good relationship between students and a teacher suddenly changes and the teacher does not know why. Therefore, it is important that teachers find out about students' points of view; that is, a teacher should see himself or herself through students' eyes. Investigate your students' feelings by using a questionnaire such as the one described here, or develop one together with your students.

Precautions and Possible Pitfalls

Just listening to students and observing their behavior doesn't give teachers all the information they need to make intelligent decisions about how to treat students. Do not feel offended if you praise, help, or encourage students and they react in a disapproving way. Older students, and especially mediocre students, often are embarrassed when treated like more ambitious students. Their embarrassment is the reason they act so aloof when praised by a teacher, but, under the surface, they often feel pleased.

SOURCE

von Hauff, R. (1982). Schüler geben ihren Lehrern Rückmeldung—Ein Rückmeldungsfragebogen, der von Grund- und Reallehrern sowie ihren Schülern entwickelt und erprobt wurde [Pupils give their teachers feedback—A feedback questionnaire developed and evaluated by teachers of primary schools and junior high schools]. *Psychologie in Erziehung und Unterricht, 29,* 167-171.

THE TIP (4.13)

 If students have poor mathematics self-concepts, implement a variety of strategies to help them feel that they can be successful learners in mathematics.

What the Research Says

Academic self-concept involves a feeling of confidence in one's ability to achieve, self-reliance, and recognition of one's strengths and weaknesses. Positive academic self-concept results from frequent and consistent success experiences in specific subjects, which are generalized to overall success in school. With repeated failure experiences, a student develops a widespread, self-defeating pattern of achievement motivation and an avoidance of failure to protect a sense of dignity. Self-concept affects a student's choice of tasks, willingness to try, persistence, and actual performance. When self-concept of ability is threatened, students may show failure-avoidance motivation. Failure-avoidance strategies include not trying, procrastinating, false effort, and even denial of effort. Failure without effort is equated to failure with honor. Self-concept is multidimensional. It has one general facet and several specific ones, for example, in specific subject areas. Many studies indicate there is almost no relationship between verbal and math self-concepts. For example, a student may feel he or she is a great reader (good reading self-concept) but is bad in math (poor math self-concept). Research suggests that such self-perceptions are formed by internal and external comparison processes. Internal comparison involves comparing oneself in different subjects, for example, "I am better in reading than I am in math." External comparison involves comparing oneself to others, "Most of the students in my class are better in math than I am."

Classroom Applications

There are many ways teachers can help improve students' academic self-concepts. For very young children, praising efforts often increase self-confidence in their ability to succeed. For older children, however, effort and ability are seen as different, so praising one's effort has a different effect. It may actually undermine confidence in ability. Techniques for improving academic self-concept can be teacher centered or student centered. Teacher-centered techniques emphasize the teacher's responsibility whereas student-centered techniques place greater emphasis on the student's responsibility.

Teacher-centered techniques:

1. Convey your positive expectations for students' performance.

2. Provide a cushion of frequent and consistent success experiences by

   a. Starting with the known/simple and moving gradually to the unknown/complex;

   b. Helping students break complex problems/tasks into reachable subgoals.

Listen to students attentively and treat them respectfully.

Student-centered techniques:

1. Encourage students to have positive expectations of their own performance and to not push themselves too hard or to be too soft.

2. Teach students to direct their self-criticism to their own correctable actions instead of themselves as people. For example, "I studied the wrong material" instead of "I'm just not good in math."

3. Help students learn to recognize their successes and to identify their patterns of successes and failures.

4. Guide students in developing action plans to translate failure experiences into strategies for improving their performance.

5. Encourage students to redefine success by exceeding their own past performance in mathematics instead of comparing themselves to others, or comparing themselves in mathematics to a subject they feel confident in.

Precautions and Possible Pitfalls

Bear in mind that not all methods work well with all students and not all teachers can implement these techniques with equal facility and effectiveness. Therefore, the teacher must select those methods that best suit him or her or best fit the intended population or individuals. It's best not to rely strictly on teacher-centered techniques. Consequently, teachers should try to stretch themselves and experiment with the student-centered techniques with which they feel most comfortable. This will help to prevent students from being dependent on the teacher for developing and maintaining their positive mathematics self-concepts. Teacher-centered techniques, when used at all, are best used when beginning to develop students' positive mathematics self-concepts. It is then best to shift to student-centered techniques.

SOURCE

Marsh, H. (1986). Verbal and math self-concepts: An internal/external frame of reference model. *American Educational Research Journal, 23*(1), 129-149.

THE TIP (4.14)

 When considering how students view themselves as mathematics students, be sensitive to possible gender differences, ethnic differences, and to the relationship between ethnicity and gender.

What the Research Says

Mathematics self-concept appears to be more complicated than general self-concept or self-concept in other school subjects. It often differs for males and females, for students from different ethnic groups, and there are differences in mathematics self-concepts for males and females depending on their ethnic background. A study was conducted with 214 students before their freshman year at a large, public urban university. Students were enrolled in a pre-freshman summer program designed to improve their academic skills to better prepare them for college. The initial sample consisted of 42% blacks, 32% Hispanics, 18% Asians, 2% whites, and 6% others. Of these, 139 were females and 75 were males. Two questionnaires were administered to students: the Thinking About Problem Solving scale (TAPS) and the Michigan State Self-Concept of Ability Scale. The TAPS measured students' reports of their higher-level thinking (metacognition) about problem solving; the self-concept scale measured students' views of themselves as learners in general and in the specific subjects of mathematics, English, science, and social studies. Mathematics was the only type of self-concept that showed significant differences in all the variables of gender, ethnicity, and the interaction between gender and ethnicity. Mathematics self-concept showed a significant positive relationship to problem-solving metacognition for blacks and Hispanics, but not for Asians.

Classroom Applications

Classrooms are increasingly characterized by ethnic diversity, and this trend will become even stronger in the next millennium. Teachers often have unconscious stereotypes of students based on their ethnicity and gender. It is very important for teachers to treat each student as an individual and to tune into and understand each student's thoughts and feelings about learning mathematics.

Precautions and Possible Pitfalls

 Beware of stereotyping students based on gender or ethnicity! Although there are general trends for girls versus boys and for students from different ethnic groups, teachers should not assume their students to have any predisposed characteristics.

SOURCE

Hartman, H., Everson, H., Tobias, S., & Gourgey, A. (1996). Self-concept and meta-cognition in ethnic minorities. *Urban Education, 31*(2), 222-238.

THE TIP (4.15)

 When thinking about how to improve students' mathematics self-concept, girls benefit from successful performance in mathematics more than boys.

What the Research Says

Self-concept is a very complex concept, much more so than originally recognized. Self-concept develops in different ways for girls than for boys. Achievement in mathematics directly affects mathematics self-concept for girls but it does not have that direct effect in boys. A study was conducted with 114 girls and 117 boys from 8 schools in a large city in Norway. One or two sixth-grade classes were randomly selected from each school. Schools were randomly selected from four zones in the city. Two questionnaires were administered to the students: the Academic Self-Esteem Scale and the Perceived Competence Scale for Children. Researchers examined the effects of mathematics and verbal achievement on general, mathematics, and verbal self-concepts. Cognitive aspects of students' verbal and mathematics self-concepts were examined in reference to students' expectations of success on 20 mathematics and 30 verbal tasks. Tasks were designed to reflect students' mathematics and verbal curricula. Academic achievement was measured by students' performance on these tasks. Boys and girls did not differ significantly in their mathematics achievement, mathematics self-concept, or general academic self-concept. They did, however, differ in how achievement affected self-concepts. Although girls showed a stronger effect of mathematics achievement on mathematics self-concept than boys, boys showed a stronger effect of verbal achievement on verbal self-concept than girls.

Classroom Applications

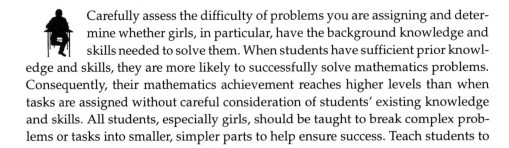 Carefully assess the difficulty of problems you are assigning and determine whether girls, in particular, have the background knowledge and skills needed to solve them. When students have sufficient prior knowledge and skills, they are more likely to successfully solve mathematics problems. Consequently, their mathematics achievement reaches higher levels than when tasks are assigned without careful consideration of students' existing knowledge and skills. All students, especially girls, should be taught to break complex problems or tasks into smaller, simpler parts to help ensure success. Teach students to

evaluate their progress in mathematics by comparing their current performance with their own previous performance instead of comparing their performance to other students.

Precautions and Possible Pitfalls

Although success is vital for improving students' (especially girls') mathematics self-concept, beware of making tasks too simple! Without challenge, students will dismiss whatever success they have, and their mathematics self-concept will not improve if the achievement comes too easily. In addition, students will get bored if tasks are too easy. By comparing their performance in mathematics to other students instead of to their own prior performance, students create a self-destructive trap that encourages them to maintain a poor view of themselves as mathematics learners.

SOURCE

Skaalvik, E. M., & Rankin, R. J. (1988). Math, verbal, and general academic self-concepts: The internal/external frame of reference model and gender differences in self-concept structure. *Journal of Educational Psychology, 82*(3), 546-554.

THE TIP (4.16)

 Help students develop self-control to enhance their thinking and independence, as well as to ease your own workload.

What the Research Says

Just a few small changes in your methodology could provide an increase in students' self-control. The increase of students' self-control does not release the teacher from his or her external control. External control by the teacher is the basic prerequisite for step-by-step cultivation of self-control. Gradually transfer your control and guidance to students as they develop their own control and feeling of responsibility. In a study about students' self-control, students reported that their lack of self-control made them feel uncertain as to whether they really reached an educational objective. That's why students want external control by the teacher, and that's precisely why teachers need to guide students in realizing self-control.

The research has shown that

1. High-achieving students have better self-control than students who have learning weaknesses. Good students, however, sometimes think that they do not need to practice self-control.

2. Preplanned self-control is hard to observe in students. When self-control is observed, it tends to be more reactive than proactive.

3. The more students are proactive in their self-control, the better they are in reacting with self-control.

4. Girls show a stronger tendency toward self-control than boys. Boys tend to skip steps toward attaining self-control or do it superficially.

5. In high stress situations (such as tests), students realize a greater degree of self-control. Self-control during homework tends to be considered as superfluous.

6. When teachers control students' behavior, students adapt to this control and refrain from self-control.

7. Teacher's efforts to encourage students' self-control seem to focus on reactive or result-related self-control.

8. Students only know about techniques of result-related or reactive self-control. These include self-checking, using reference books, using calculators, or verifying the results of a calculation. Low-achieving students tended to mention verifying a calculation as the technique of self-control. Only a few high-achieving students identified making rough estimates as a technique of proactive self-control.

Classroom Applications

 Practice continuous methods of self-control such as

- Making rough estimates (do not trust blindly in the calculator!)
- Using mathematical theorems
- Making drawings to represent mathematical ideas
- Drawing graphs to represent mathematical concepts
- Using templates and measuring instruments

Practical ways for step-by-step improvements in students' self-control include the following:

- Students make mutual comparisons of their answers and solution strategies
- If a student presents his or her way of solving a problem, another student should give the problem solver feedback
- Combine assignments with elements of playful self-control. This is suitable particularly for students with learning weaknesses or students with impulsive work habits
- Give assignments that force students to engage in proactive self-control:
  - Design a task that contains superfluous information
  - Assign a problem or task that is not solvable or is only solvable under certain conditions

With each of these self-control techniques, a teacher is likely to complain about the time involved. Developing students' self-control abilities will, however, save time in the long run.

Precautions and Possible Pitfalls

 Strict demands on students to use techniques of self-control incessantly or indiscriminately can backfire. If a student already understood an algorithmic procedure, he or she will view the demanded checking only as a mechanical (and thereby meaningless) activity. As a result, the student may devalue self-control.

SOURCE

Fischer, F., & Bernd, K. (1991). Ergebnisse von Untersuchungen zur Selbstkontrolle bei Schülern der 7. Klasse im Mathematikunterricht [Results of research about the self-control of seventh-grade students in math classes]. *Mathematik in der Schule, 29*(11), 761-768.

Index

EDITOR'S NOTE: Page references followed by *f* indicate figures.